THE
GREAT WAR
HANDBOOK

THE GREAT WAR HANDBOOK

A GUIDE FOR FAMILY HISTORIANS & STUDENTS OF THE CONFLICT

GEOFF BRIDGER

FOREWORD BY
CORRELLI BARNETT

Pen & Sword
FAMILY HISTORY

First published in Great Britain in 2009 by
PEN & SWORD FAMILY HISTORY
an imprint of
Pen & Sword Books Ltd
47 Church Street
Barnsley
South Yorkshire
S70 2AS

ISBN 978 1 84415 936 9

A CIP catalogue record for this book is
available from the British Library.

Typeset in Palatino and Optima by
S L Menzies-Earl

Printed and bound in England by
CPI UK

Pen & Sword Books Ltd incorporates the imprints of
Pen & Sword Aviation, Pen & Sword Maritime, Pen & Sword Military,
Wharncliffe Local History, Pen & Sword Select, Pen & Sword Military Classics
and Leo Cooper

For a complete list of Pen & Sword titles please contact
PEN & SWORD BOOKS LTD
47 Church Street, Barnsley, South Yorkshire, S70 2AS, England
E-mail: enquiries@pen-and-sword.co.uk
Website: www.pen-and-sword.co.uk

CONTENTS

LIST OF TABLES

FOREWORD

I warmly recommend *The Great War Handbook* to all those wishing to brief themselves factually about this titanic conflict. It will prove especially valuable as background information to families researching into the wartime service of an ancestor. It will act as an essential resource for those either teaching in school about the war or guiding school parties round the battlefields and war cemeteries. For young people, *The Great War Handbook* will provide a fascinating but objective starting-point for their reading.

Geoff Bridger has done us all – professional historians included – a great service.

Correlli Barnett CBE
National President, the Western Front Association.

* * *

ACKNOWLEDGEMENTS

Much of the material for this book comes from my own research notes for talks I have been giving for very many years. And much of that, in turn, originated from veterans of the Great War. I have been most privileged to speak to many former soldiers, sailors and airmen – some relations, some friends of my father who served from 1 September 1914 until 19 February 1919 and other veterans who kindly tolerated my persistent questioning. Those priceless interviews took place over several decades, mostly whilst the veterans were still relatively young and their memories fresh and accurate. Many kindly gave me copies of their precious photographs and documents at the time and some are reproduced in this book.

There are various institutions without whose help and cooperation a book of this kind would be impossible. During the course of my research I visited many archives, institutions, libraries and museums but wish to specially mention: The National Archives at Kew, The Commonwealth War Graves Commission, The Imperial war Museum, Lambeth, London, The National Army Museum, Chelsea, London. The staff of all these organizations are always most professional and unstinting with their help.

I wish to thank for their help: The eminent military historian Correlli Barnett for kindly agreeing to write the foreword and for many invaluable suggestions to improve the book; Rupert Harding, my commissioning editor, for general guidance, tolerance and encouragement; Jane Robson, my copy-editor, for her expertise in spotting and correcting my non-deliberate mistakes; Sue Rowland for whose cartographic skills I am indebted – she has modified and made readable old maps and converted my scribbles into useful graphics; Julian Sykes, for information on his specialist subject – mortars; Terry Whippy for supplying items and photographs from his collection for examination and photographing; Bill Fulton and the Machine Gun Corps Association for help in defining the Corps – not the simplest of tasks.

And my thanks to many friends for words of wisdom, encouragement and advice on several subjects. They include: Chris Buckland, Gary Buckland, Terry Cave, Gary Cooper, Bernard Delsert, Meurig Jones, Henry Lequien, Hilary Llewellyn-Williams, Julian Putkowski, Guy Smith, Angela Wiseman and Paul Yates.

I am especially indebted to my old friend Paul Reed. He and I have trudged many a battlefield over the years and his knowledge and expertise on matters concerning the Great War are truly formidable. He kindly glanced over my manuscript and made several helpful and valuable suggestions. I naturally accept full responsibility for any residual faux pas, errors and omissions.

Writing a book is, in my case, a long and laborious task, which has been made so much easier by the willing cooperation and unstinting help of my wonderful wife and friend Anna-May. She has been totally supportive in my endeavours and encouraged me to continue on those 'dark days'. She has offered many valuable words of advice concerning my phraseology; excused unfortunate phraseology levelled at my temperamental computer and accepted my excuses for not helping with the housework or garden for a long time. Thank you Anna-May. I could not have done it without you.

DEDICATION

This book is dedicated to all the soldiers, sailors and airmen of the Great War who faithfully served their country in time of crisis.

I would especially like to remember my cousin, Lance-Corporal Harry Bridger, 2/Essex Regiment, who was killed in action on 18 November 1914.

Lance-Corporal Harry Bridger, 2/Essex Regt.

INTRODUCTION

This book is not another history of the Great War, although it does include a brief account of its origins and main events. As its title suggests, it is primarily designed to answer many of the basic questions newcomers, and indeed experienced historians, often ask when confronted by this enormous and challenging subject. With so many books and other media being available on specific aspects of the Great War, this guide should prove to be useful for students, family historians, teachers and anyone who is eager to gain an all-round understanding of the nature of the conflict. Existing books, many excellent in themselves, tend to concentrate on regiments, individuals, places or battles. Rarely do they explain what it was like to be in the firing line.

The handbook will help provide a greater understanding of what servicemen went through. It can be used either on its own or as a companion to other material you may be studying, to help interpret the many terms and jargon used. It covers not only what happened and why, but what the Great War was like for ordinary soldiers who were, often unwillingly, caught up in it. Sections describe the conditions soldiers endured, the deadly risks they ran, their daily routines and the small roles they played in the complex military machine they were part of. Most aspects of the soldier's life, from recruitment and training, through life in the trenches, the equipment they used, to the experience of battle and its appalling aftermath are considered. It does not however go into the minutiae of equipment nor give details of battles or the battalions that fought them. The contents show exactly what is covered and, if desired, the reader can go straight to the subject on which they seek clarification.

Most measurements are quoted in imperial, as used at the time, but as so many modern students are more accustomed to metric I have added the *approximate* equivalent in parentheses where thought appropriate. As will be seen from the weights involved, the Army did not 'do light'. Everything was built to be 'soldier proof' and very durable. Soldiers had a great deal of heavy equipment to carry about.

When describing certain pieces of equipment, to save space I often give examples of perhaps two of the most commonly encountered items. The interested reader wishing to know more about other variations should refer to the many excellent specialist publications available on the market. Some of these are referred to in the Bibliography. Aspects of a subject may appear in more than one chapter so it is always worth consulting the index.

As with everything else in life there are exceptions to many rules and I ask for the indulgence of any specialist who challenges any unqualified statement of mine as necessarily definitive. For example, I refer to sappers being trained to fight if necessary. Some miners (sappers) went straight to the front, or rather beneath it, with little or no military training. It is not always practical to list every exception.

From the British perspective the 1914–18 war was the first ever conflict to involve virtually everybody in the country. In one form or other the First World War was just that. It spanned most of the globe. And our gallant servicemen died on operations that reached from the Falklands in the South Atlantic to north China in Asia. However, by far the greatest number who served – and perhaps were wounded or died – did so on the Western Front upon which this work concentrates. It is also weighted towards the army and especially the infantry, as it was after all they, with a lot of help from chums in many other units, who won the war! Nevertheless, the various other theatres of war are considered and brief details of the activities there are recounted. We must not forget the sailors and airmen who contributed to the Allied victory and so often lost their lives or limbs in the process. Consequently a very brief summary of their part in the conflict is also included.

The weapons of war were specifically designed to kill as efficiently as possible and were used with equal effect on land, sea and air no matter where on earth fighting occurred. The terrain, weather and conditions varied of course but suffering and casualties, both human and animal, are the inevitable outcome of the war. Despite its full title 'The Great War for Civilisation' there is no such thing as a civilized war.

The conditions for men and animals were, by today's standards, harsh or even brutal. Punishment for wrongdoers was swift and uncompromising. But, as amplified in Chapter 3 we must accept that the men and women who served in our armed forces, and indeed in the munitions factories at home, did so in a very different environment from that prevailing today. And, not having the benefit of our hindsight, did so more or less willingly. That is not to say there were no disputes. There were, but with a few exceptions these mainly related to pay and not the conditions of the time.

Today the First and Second World Wars are taught in schools as history, not as recent memory. The teachers and pupils can have no first-, or

The thirteenth-century Cloth Hall in Ypres was totally destroyed by shell fire by 1918.

probably even second-hand, experience of the Great War. Reminiscences of veterans, if not already recorded, have been lost forever. But that does not mean all evidence is gone – far from it. Family history is one of the most popular pastimes of our age, with so much information from old records being transcribed and made available either on the internet or other easy access forms. Family history societies abound and have large libraries of data for their members. Our quest for information about our forefathers seems unlimited. For the greater part, however, all we can discover are basic facts such as dates and places of birth, marriage and death. It is rare to be able to discover what sort of life our forebears led. We do though know what conditions were like during the Great War and if, as is the case in the majority of British families, a member served in the armed forces we can discover what it was like to be there.

Research sources will be covered later but if you are investigating a particular individual or unit then it is best to adopt certain basic techniques at an early stage. Gather whatever evidence is available and record it systematically. The trusted notebook and pencil are essential tools. Even second-hand stories from the children of veterans have their place. But be prepared to challenge everything you have recorded. Even official documents and records contain errors. Demand evidence but do not be disappointed if it is not immediately available. Put it in the temporary 'unproven but interesting if only it is true' file. Hopefully much of it will slot into place eventually.

Do not give up hope in your research, for unexpected gems resurface every so often to provide that missing piece of family history. It is worth checking exactly what relevant items are hidden away in the attic of any descendants of Great War soldiers, sailors or airmen. Items such as photographs, documents, letters from the Front and medals were often thought worthless just after the war and put away and forgotten. They can be vital to your quest and advice on interpreting them and other heirlooms and artefacts will be offered. It may well be beneficial to join your local family history society to not only gain tips on research, but also to share with their members your own story and any treasures you have discovered.

Although many sources of information are available and can be consulted, unfortunately large numbers of records have been irretrievably lost or destroyed over the years. Additionally it is appropriate to say here that no record of what each soldier did on a day-by-day basis exists or ever has existed. Where service documents survive they commonly indicate physical descriptions and family details, together with limited health and discipline notes and sometimes movement between units. Perhaps surprisingly, for those who died there is often more information available than for those who lived. It is however quite reasonable to assume that a soldier in any particular unit enjoyed the same conditions and privations as his chums. And many of these have been chronicled in considerable detail over the years. It is from the plethora of books, documents, photographs and official records that much of the data in this book is condensed. Other sources include my own background notes to talks I have been giving for very many years.

Vital information, perhaps seemingly trivial but still essential to the greater understanding of what it was really like, has been derived from the statements made by veterans. And that includes my own father. Whereas the correct use of the bayonet is described in detail in infantry training manuals, I know of no contemporary publication, official or otherwise, that describes accurately how it felt to be infested with lice. 'How to scratch' was most definitely not covered in King's Regulations. The fact that toilet paper was not issued to the ordinary soldier failed to be mentioned in the surfeit

Re-examination of the negative with a magnifying class reveals parts of the inscription. Searching Soldiers Died in the Great War *shows the casualty to be Sapper Frank Vickery, killed in action, 16 Aug. 1917.*

of, often quite useless, forms and instructions that were regularly sent to the front line every day. But perhaps those forms were rather useful after all!

Throughout the book the terms, 'men', 'soldier', 'serviceman', 'troops', are used, which seems to imply that only males were involved in the Great War. That is simply not true. If it were not for the millions of women involved at home in hazardous war-related jobs, the conflict could not have continued. We must also remember with pride the thousands of women who were in war zones engaged in nursing and related occupations. Several lost their lives in the process; many more caught nasty illnesses or were injured. And all were in danger. During the First World War women did not fight in a combat role in the British Forces and it is not therefore appropriate to use such modern terms as 'serviceperson'. The soldiers were men after all. In addition, unless separately amplified, the terms 'men', 'soldier', etc. include both officers and other ranks.

The First World War was a learning war. In the majority of earlier conflicts the generals could control the battle from a central position by signalling their intentions. Adequate communication was simply not possible over the large broken battlefields. Portable radio equipment was awaiting invention. And hindsight did not exist. Technology was advancing at an alarming rate, as it invariably does in wartime, but no experience existed as to the best ways to employ it. The eminent military historian John Terrain summarized the situation: 'It was the only war that has ever been fought without voice control. Generals became impotent at the very moment when they would expect and be expected to display their greatest proficiency.'

We must never forget it was also a deadly war. In simplistic terms, one out of every five soldiers who served at the Front was killed and a further two were injured during the war.

We will Remember them.

Chapter 1

PROLOGUE AND OVERVIEW OF THE WAR

The history of the Great War, especially its famous battles, has already been well chronicled by eminent historians. In consequence I here place greater emphasis on the less well-publicized origins and opening moves rather than the overall cataclysm. The full political considerations and military operations of the war are naturally outside the scope of this book anyway.

The fighting in the various theatres of war other than France and Belgium was often intense and cost many lives. And yet the final outcome of the war would only be decided on the Western Front. Whilst the other theatres of war (often called, I feel disrespectfully, 'side-shows') are briefly covered, the main emphasis in this short narrative is devoted to the Western Front. With the full realization that it was a world war involving so many nations, the main focus is on the British involvement because of space constraints. Sadly, even then only a very brief summary is possible.

Prelude to War

The name Gavrilo Princip will be familiar to many students of the Great War. It was he after all, a disaffected 19-year-old consumptive youth, who fired those fatal shots in Sarajevo on 28 June 1914.

Princip was part of a disparate Serbian nationalist gang optimistically recruited, armed and despatched by Colonel Dragutin Dimitrijević, head of the Serbian military intelligence and the terrorist group 'Black Hand'. Their

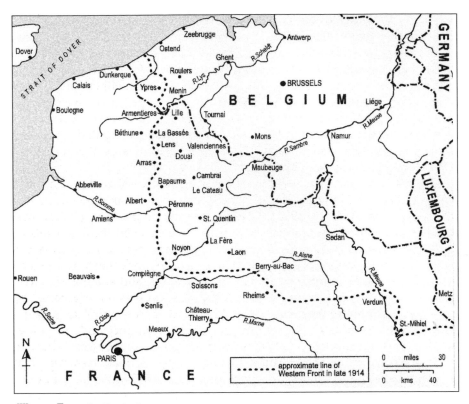

Western Front. Sue Rowland

mission was to assassinate Archduke Ferdinand, the heir presumptive to the Austrian-Hungarian Empire and a man deeply opposed to Serbian nationalism. Sophie, the Archduke's wife, was also shot dead – an unnecessary act for she had no political or royal standing at all.

The spectacular assassination has been called the 'fuse that set Europe ablaze' but that was a slight exaggeration in terms. It certainly did not calm the situation but it was by no means the sole or even principal cause of the First World War. One has to look further back and further afield than that.

What is true is that the immediate origins of the First World War stem from the volatile area we loosely call 'the Balkans'. It was (and still is) populated by very many different ethnic groups, which basically did not get on with each other for numerous historical reasons that dated back centuries. The same was true of the once great Austro-Hungarian Empire, which by 1914 was losing its grip on power, but still had ambitions in the region where many alliances and much intrigue prevailed. Those ambitions were really above its military capability, for its standing army by 1914 had dwindled to about 400,000 – small by European standards of the day. It was not very well equipped with modern field artillery either. Because of internal politics between Austria and Hungary the army had not expanded adequately to keep pace with European rivals and its reserves were small. Along with recently semi-independent Balkan states it wanted a share of the retreating Ottoman Empire, most especially towards the southeast. Unfortunately, Serbia was in the way.

Austria-Hungary had already antagonized the Russians by arbitrarily annexing Bosnia-Herzegovina in 1908. Russia, still weak after losing the Russo-Japanese War of 1904/5 could do little more than protest and harbour resentment on that occasion. Serbia too disliked the colonization, which blocked its own aspirations for an Adriatic port. As Bosnia had a large Slav population, Serbia considered she, and not Austria-Hungary, should rule there. Serbia was already an expanding and antagonistic state as a result of two Balkan Wars in 1912 and 1913 and was not frightened by its large neighbour to the north that had kept out of those conflicts. Austria-Hungary, by contrast, was nervous of potential conflict and the wider implications of regional war without the full support of a powerful backer.

The assassination of Archduke Ferdinand by Serbian terrorists was largely an attempt to show solidarity with the Serbs in Bosnia-Herzegovina. It was also to raise the profile of Serbia, whose ambitions were to reclaim as much as possible of its old empire, which had been lost to the Ottoman Empire long before. Tensions were running high.

Earlier policy decisions to implement fresh alliances for Austria-Hungary were delegated to ambitious and volatile Foreign Ministry officials, among whom were Franz von Matscheko and Alexander Graf von Hoyos. The initial policy document was not too confrontational, but matters escalated considerably following the assassination of the Archduke. The whole blame for that was laid fairly and squarely upon Serbia and the greatest proponent for swift retaliatory action against it was the chief of the general staff, Franz Conrad von Hötzendorff. He was a man of great ambition and personal drive but limited intellect. Diplomatic meetings between Austria-Hungary and Germany were hurriedly arranged and much spin was brought into the situation. The actions of Dimitrijević's men at Sarajevo did not represent the Serbian government's official position, although there was much public support for the assassination.

Central Powers

By the time of the First World War there were already two powerful alliances or understandings that had evolved in Europe. One was between Germany and Austria-Hungary – sometimes called the Central Powers. It was signed in 1879 to provide mutual support in case a peeved France or an unstable Russia attacked either country. France was still peeved following its loss of the provinces Alsace and Lorraine in 1871 after its defeat in the Franco-Prussian War of 1870/1. Russia wanted to expand into the Balkans. Italy joined Germany and Austria-Hungary to form the Triple Alliance in 1882. It joined because France had seized Tunisia, in which Italy had considerable interest, the previous year. As a latecomer, Germany lacked much in the way of overseas colonies when compared to France, Britain and other colonial powers. It was disturbed by the potential of the Royal Navy to cut off its supply of vital materials from neutral countries in the event of hostilities. Germany was however a rapidly expanding industrial country, most especially since the unification of its various states in 1871. Its steel and coal production had increased far more than that of its rivals. Much of this was used in the armaments industry to create a first-class, well-organized, well-equipped and well-trained army and also rapidly increase the size and quality of its fleet – the last element a cause of great concern to the British.

The ambivalent Italy used a technicality to avoid actual fighting on behalf of the Triple Alliance of which she was a member. Instead she declared neutrality in August 1914 and waited to be tempted with promises of territory by the Allies in May 1915 before joining them. She declared war on Turkey on 20 August 1915 but waited until 27 August the following year before declaring war on Germany.

Turkey too was somewhat ambivalent until very late in the day. Both Britain and Germany had input in the region mainly for economic and political rather than militaristic reasons. Turkey was not considered initially by either Britain or Germany as a good military partner. Turkey however needed an ally in the area to bolster its own prestige. Then, in 1914, Britain made a series of diplomatic blunders which offended Turkey, whilst Germany made all the right noises – and backed these up with arms and naval supplies. Finally, antagonized by Britain, Turkey decided to join the Great War on the side of the Central Powers.

The Allies

The other European grouping was the Triple Entente. This grouping was often referred to as the 'Allies' that other countries, such as the United States of America, joined in due course. It started as an alliance between

France and Russia in 1894 to confront the Triple Alliance after the latter's formation in 1882. Britain joined with France in 1904 to form the Entente Cordiale – mainly to combat the perceived menace from the expanding German fleets. Britain finally linked up with Russia in 1907 and the Triple Entente was formed. Britain also had a treaty with Japan that released British warships from the Pacific region. It was left to the Japanese Navy to deal with any enemy merchantmen and warships that wished to trade and roam there. There were other, earlier alliances between the various nations that have little bearing on the Great War and are not discussed here.

The German and French nations by 1914 were disproportionate in the size of their populations. France had about 40 million people whereas Germany, at around 65 million, had over one third more. The difference gave Germany a considerable advantage in the number of men it could potentially recruit into its armed forces. Perhaps surprisingly, in 1914 both countries had similarly sized armies at around 3 million men each, once reservists were recalled. But this ratio was unsustainable in the long term.

The prospect of Germany having to fight on two fronts was highly likely in view of the alliance between France and Russia. We must also remember that, as Poland had effectively been annexed by Russia, the distances between the outer Russian borders and France through Germany had shrunk to around 520 miles – a day's troop-train journey. Despite naval rivalries, and diplomatic incidents, war with Britain was not considered too likely. Britain was rather preoccupied with problems in Ireland where home rule was the major issue and had the potential for violence. It had a very small army and was not too concerned with developments in the Balkans, which would probably be localized. Germany was however concerned about France, especially as two incidents in Morocco had raised the tension between those countries. A further incident at Agadir in 1911 did nothing to lessen the tension and had the potential to involve Britain, as intimated by Lloyd George's Mansion House speech that year. The competitive search for sustainable overseas markets by the European powers did nothing to ease the background tensions.

Austria-Hungary might be able to defeat Serbia but she could not survive unaided if Russia intervened on behalf of her Slavic kin. She sought help and backing from Germany if she was challenged by Russia. And got it. The so-called 'blank cheque', evidently approved by the Kaiser and senior ministers, was soon to be cashed by Austria-Hungary. Meetings were rapidly arranged between von Hoyos and various ministers from Austria and Hungary. They were often fed cleverly distorted versions of the true nature of German support. Eventually agreement upon the next course of action, war against Serbia, was approved. A forty-eight-hour ultimatum was sent to Serbia, the terms of which, it was believed, would give Serbia no option but to reject them and thus commit her to war. Intelligence sources were of the opinion that Russia was not yet militarily ready for war. There was also the naively optimistic idea that the slightly fragile Triple Entente might not hold together. There were yet other nationalistic reasons why Germany was not particularly opposed to a limited war which might increase its world influence and at the same time unite factions at home, where socialist unrest threatened disorder.

In fact Serbia accepted virtually all of the conditions of the ultimatum. It therefore gained a slight diplomatic advantage to help counteract the negative international feelings towards it following the assassination of the grand duke. On 24 July 1914, as well as protesting her innocence in the assassinations, Serbia made a direct appeal to the Tsar for Russian assistance. Amazingly, in an official statement on 27 July 1914, Sir Edward Grey, the British Foreign Secretary, sided fully with Austria, to the extent of stating that he regarded the Serbian response as inadequate and would not blame Austria-Hungary for any military action they might take. In view of the tension, and as a precaution against a pre-emptive Austria-Hungarian strike, Serbia set about mobilizing its own forces. Austria-Hungary was so convinced that their ultimatum would be rejected out of hand, thus wrong-footing Serbia, that they too ordered mobilization. Last-minute efforts by Germany to exercise restraint went unheeded and Austria-Hungary declared war and then, without more ado, opened fire on Serbia on 28 July 1914.

In earlier times countries often mobilized – that is, got ready for war but did not actually fight – as a means of posturing and brinkmanship. That was all very well between small countries in localized situations. It was not so easy when maybe millions of men were involved. It took time for a country to get ready for war. The standing army had to be reinforced with reserves. Reservists were trained soldiers who had served their time in uniform, were released to their homes and civilian occupations, but subject to recall at times of crisis. Men could be on a reserve or recall list for thirty years or more and this feature of continental armies meant that huge forces could be assembled relatively quickly. The reservists however had to be notified and respond to their call-up, taken to their assembly areas, given uniforms, equipment and arms. And possibly retrained. Then the reinforced armies had to proceed to their designated concentration areas ready for war. If war did not occur, the country would have been severely disrupted at considerable unnecessary expense. In practice by 1914, general mobilization was tantamount to war. If your hostile neighbour was ready and poised across the border, that threat could not be ignored and had to be countered. All that was required was the formal declaration. Existing treaties and alliances virtually ensured that once one country started mobilization or offensive action against another the domino effect would soon set in.

War, from Britain's perspective, was becoming increasingly likely day by day but the weak Liberal Government needed to be persuaded it was inevitable. The Cabinet was split on whether to fight or not. Much last-minute diplomacy by Sir Edward Grey was conducted, until finally the German invasion of Belgium gave Britain the valid reason it required to declare war on Germany. Many countries including Britain and indeed Prussia (Germany) had pledged support for Belgian neutrality as far back as 1839. The violation of her neutrality was the last straw. Germany had not thought Britain would oppose its actions in Belgium, which it regarded as fundamental in its battle with France. It was surprised and dismayed that Britain did not agree. The First World War, in all its horrors, finally commenced from a British perspective at 11pm (midnight in Berlin) on 4 August 1914. Last-minute ultimatums to Germany to withdraw from Belgium were rejected.

As we have seen in the birth of the two major alliances, the causes of the unease and suspicion that prevailed in pre-war Europe did not all come from the Balkans, even though it was there that hostilities commenced. Indeed friction in Europe went back many more years but here we are only considering the most recent causes of the war. Once a stone is cast into a pond it is virtually impossible to stop the ripples spreading outwards until the bank is reached or breached.

And as for Princip – the man accused of starting it all – he was thwarted in a suicide bid after the shooting, arrested and subjected to forceful handling. His trial and conviction for murder soon followed. As he was too young to be executed he received a twenty-year prison sentence to be served under very harsh conditions. His health soon failed, an arm had to be amputated, and he died of tuberculosis on 28 April 1918 still in prison. His grave was not marked.

The gun used by Princip now reposes in the Heeresgeschichtliches Museum in Vienna, Austria, together with the car in which the victims were shot. That fateful car had a very chequered career before ending its days in the museum. What is rather poignant is its registration number: 'A 111 118'. With a little imagination that translates to A (perhaps for Armistice) 11 11 18 or 11 November (19)18 – the date of the Armistice, and when the shooting in Europe ended. So, the car that arguably witnessed the first shots of the Great War bears the date of the last shots!

The Western Front – Plans

Germany's war plans were to rapidly defeat France and then, using its superb railway network, switch troops to the east to fight Russia. To beat France it was intended to implement the Schlieffen Plan, first drawn up in 1905 but then diluted many times. By 1914, under Schlieffen's successor von Moltke, two key elements of the original plan were no longer an option. In very simple terms the original plan involved invading France in the north by penetrating neutral Belgium via the southern appendage of equally neutral Holland. The heavily fortified and defended frontier separating France and Germany would therefore be by-passed. The northern German armies would be massively weighted in favour of their sweeping invasion leaving weaker forces to face the French across their joint frontiers further south. It was originally assumed the French would, once war had commenced, push their armies directly into Germany through Alsace and Lorraine. The intention was that the weaker German forces there would give ground, as expensively in French lives as possible, whilst occupying the attention of the bulk of the French armies.

Meanwhile the overwhelmingly powerful attack to the north would rapidly sweep in an arc around Paris and end up behind the French forces, thus trapping them between the two German army groups. This plan evolved in two major and vital ways. First, it was decided not to invade through Holland, so that Germany would continue to have access to world markets during the war via a neutral country. That was a good idea but meant that the invading Germans had much further to travel. They now had to journey round the protruding Limburg appendage to avoid infringing Holland's territory. And we must remember this was largely a pedestrian war. The second important change to the original plan was that the defensive armies facing the French across Alsace and Lorraine should not give ground after all but face up to the French. They were to be reinforced by taking soldiers from the northern invading armies. The net result was that the northern invading armies were not strong enough to fulfil their mission. This defeated the very purpose of the invasion, although vast numbers of French soldiers were killed attempting to force

FIRST CONTEMPTIBLE : "D'you remember halting here on the retreat, George?'
SECOND DITTO : "Can't call it to mind, somehow. Was it that little village in the wood there down by the river, or was it that place with the cathedral and all them factories?"

With villages razed to the ground, how true the sentiment is.

through the German lines in Alsace and Lorraine using their Plan XVII.

The French War Plan XVII was no better than the previous sixteen plans. In fact it was a catastrophe. It involved sending four-fifths of all available French soldiers in frontal attacks against well-defended German positions in Alsace, Lorraine and in the southern Ardennes. Their objective was to recapture provinces lost to Germany in 1871. The optimistic idea was to pin the Germans against the Rhine and slaughter them. But that did not happen, for the Germans were far too strong. The only tactic was élan – the bold, almost suicidal, dash into combat expected from the French soldiers against a formidable foe. The disastrous action became known as the Battle of the Frontiers and cost France dearly. By the end of November 1914 France had lost 454,000 dead – one third of their total dead for the entire war, as examination of war memorials in France will testify. Disastrously, during that time, a high proportion of all available French officers were killed or wounded, which robbed France of much needed leadership in the years to come.

The Western Front – War

On the Western Front the Great War actually commenced on 4 August when the first German soldiers violated Belgian territory. That action overshadowed the conflict in the Balkans and finally set Europe ablaze.

Britain sent an expeditionary force to war in France under the command of Field Marshal Sir John French. It consisted of one cavalry and four infantry divisions, comprising around 81,000 men. Reinforcements rapidly followed. It was to concentrate on the left of the French Fifth Army near the town of Maubeuge, close to the Belgian border and less than twelve miles south of Mons.

Although it had been observed during the Russo-Japanese War of 1905, the possibility of trench warfare in France was considered most unlikely in 1914. Long-range, accurate rifle fire by the infantry, supported by light field guns and the cavalry, seemed the most likely course of events.

The British Expeditionary Force (BEF) moved to intercept German units approaching Mons and was soon in action. Faced with overwhelming odds the British first fought, then delayed, then were forced to retreat from massed German battalions, which had already overcome spirited Belgian resistance. And that despite having marched several hundreds of kilometres from their bases in Germany. The retreat started on 23 August 1914 and lasted until 5 September, during which time the British soldiers were fighting rearguard actions and surviving as best they could. They crossed the River Aisne and then the River Marne before halting, tired, hungry and footsore, within twenty miles of Paris.

Poorly equipped British sailors, in the recently formed Royal Naval Division, attempted unsuccessfully to aid Belgian forces in the defence of Antwerp in October 1914. Many escaped to the Netherlands where they were interned for the rest of the war.

Any invading army is at a disadvantage when it comes to resupply. It can only carry limited amounts of food, fuel and munitions. Fresh stocks have to be brought through hostile territory over an ever-increasing distance. The transport system itself uses fuel and food even if it does not have to fight. A retreating army within its own country falls back on rear-based supplies and the population is generally friendly. The Germans effectively advanced, over the River Marne, to the point of exhaustion. They were low on munitions, food and other essential materials. Even the soldiers' boots were worn out. Their retreat to a place of entrenchment was inevitable. They chose to fall back on the north bank of the River Aisne and stand their ground in an easily defensible position. After a brief but bloody battle the

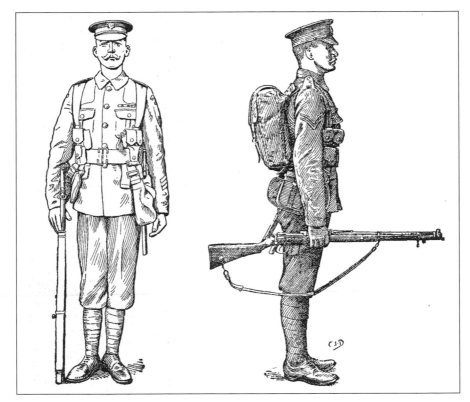

Infantryman 1914 (front).   *Infantryman 1914 (profile).*

British Expeditionary Force entrained for the Ypres Salient in Belgium leaving the French to face the enemy across the Aisne. The BEF, still small in numbers, took over part of that infamous salient and remained there for the rest of the war. Gradually it assumed responsibility for more and more of the front-line in Belgium and France. Thus the periods of stagnation, which became known as 'trench warfare', commenced. The length of the front-line in France and Belgium for which the British were responsible varied from an average of 25 miles in 1914 to over 123 miles in 1918. To carry the vast amounts of war materials required from dockside to railheads, nearly 5,000 miles of railway track were laid, including over 3,000 miles of broad gauge. Great use was also made of the canal system in Northern France for moving supplies.

Following Britain's declaration of war, the Dominions and Colonies, including Australia, Canada, India, Newfoundland, New Zealand, South Africa and other parts of the old empire, rapidly sent contingents of fighting men to help. Not all fought initially on the Western Front but all made great sacrifices during the course of the war.

By mid-October 1914, both sides were busy creating a fortified system of trenches and other obstacles that was to stretch from the North Sea to the Swiss border. From then until 21 March 1918, when the Germans launched their Spring Offensive, the opposing armies faced each other across No Man's Land. The line they created was designed to be impregnable and was defended by literally millions of well-armed and determined men. Each side launched battles against the other in an attempt to break the deadlock and it cost them dearly. None was sufficiently decisive to force the other out of the war. A list of those battles involving British forces appears in Chapter 11 and they can be studied in depth in other publications. During that period of the war hundreds of thousands of lives were lost or ruined by fighting that achieved remarkably little else. But what was the alternative?

Generals are criticized for those casualties, but the ability to foresee the future, and the technology it would bring, was impossible. And our gift of hindsight was not available to the leaders of the time! Let us briefly examine the situation. The Allies wanted the Germans out of their territories and the Germans wanted to stay. Neither was prepared to compromise. Any negotiated ceasefire during the war would effectively have resulted in a German 'win'. True they might have stopped fighting but they would not have retreated to their own borders. Why should they? They were in situ in France and Belgium and not intending to return home empty-handed. The Allies were faced with the situation of forcing them to retreat or surrender. But the German armies were well trained, well armed, well motivated, well entrenched and enshrined in the belief embossed on their belt buckles, 'Gott Mit Uns' (God with us). There were many problems in trying to force them to leave that need to be considered:

- By diplomacy: we have already considered this – unlikely to succeed.
- By the blockade of Germany: yes, this works and was adopted from the start, but Germany was or became largely self-sufficient in most things and it takes a very long time to starve a whole country into submission.
- Attack in other areas such as the Mediterranean and the Middle East: this was tried and found wanting. The only decisive area of conflict remained the Western Front.

• Go round the German lines. But where? Before the trench lines were finally established each side had attempted to outflank the other. The barrier was however completed and stretched, effectively unbroken, for around 450 miles (720km). It is difficult to be precise as it did not follow roads or easily measured features of the land. It evolved wherever the fighting stalled and men dug in. It zigzagged around natural obstacles, formed salients and changed considerably during the war.

To the north was the North Sea. Invasion by seaborne landing craft was considered but abandoned as impractical. It is immensely difficult to land a large army from the sea without purpose-built ships and massive preliminary destruction of the enemy coastal defences. Landing craft, as used in the Second World War, had yet to be invented. Then there is the problem of rapid movement if and when ashore and the whole question of resupply.

To the south was Switzerland, a fiercely neutral and easily defended mountainous country completely unsuitable for rapid movement of invading troops. If it were easy the Germans would have tried it! As it happened neither side wanted to even consider the possibility. Switzerland was far too valuable as a neutral country with which to trade and exchange men, messages and espionage.

• By tunnelling underneath No Man's Land into German-held territory. We did extensive tunnelling on the Western Front but those tunnels were mostly narrow excavations designed for the placing of mines to destroy specific targets. They were totally unsuitable for the movement of hundreds of thousands of invading soldiers carrying all sorts of weapons and equipment. And each side could usually detect the other's tunnelling activities and take countermeasures.

• By going over the lines. How? Paratroops were way into the future. Even if the idea had occurred to someone, the parachutes of the day were unsuitable for carrying heavily armed men. And the aeroplanes were not powerful enough to carry much weight.

So what are we left with? We cannot go round the enemy. We cannot go beneath him. We cannot drop soldiers behind him. Surely the only other way remaining is to go through him! As we have seen, the lines were strong and heavily defended. Any frontal attack, with the weapons, equipment and communications (or rather lack of) at the time was inevitably going to be very costly in human lives. Once a preplanned attack commenced there was no quick or practical way for high command to communicate with its own forces. Truly portable radios and mobile phones did not exist. A local commander could not quickly call off or redirect an artillery barrage from his forward position. He could not get reinforcements to his aid without much delay. He could not retreat without endangering adjacent battalions. He probably could not even call his own men above the din of battle. He had to make do with what had been planned and with what he had available. Even when allowed to use his own initiative and deviate from the plan (not always a good idea, for units on either side would be unaware of the change) he had little scope beyond minor local skirmishes.

New weapons and tactics evolved as the war progressed. Poison gas, flamethrowers and tanks were born here but none was capable of winning the war. Aircraft design leapt forward at an amazing pace. Suitable countermeasures were found. War is a great time for rapid advances in technology and this growth really began with the Great War. It was a learning war, for nothing like it had ever occurred before. The British Army had effectively been a police force keeping order throughout the Empire before the war. Britain expected the war to be mobile, as experienced in the South African War. We had no experience or training for a continental war involving millions of men dug in and resisting eviction. Our Belgian and French allies, later joined by American troops, fought alongside us in many brave and costly actions such as that at Verdun.

Scene of devastation in Chateau Wood, Oct 1917. The duckboards were essential. Many men drowned in this type of quagmire.

What broke the stalemate? Well it was actually the Germans. They had been fighting a war on two main fronts more or less simultaneously until the Russians sought peace at the end of 1917. There had been little fighting on the Eastern Front between March and September 1917, in anticipation of Russian capitulation in an atmosphere of Revolution. An armistice was agreed in December 1917 and was followed by a Peace Treaty between Russia and the Central Powers in March 1918. This treaty wrested vast territories from Russia but necessitated Germany keeping a considerable number of troops in the area as insurance against resumed hostilities. Nevertheless around one million men were released for service on the Western Front in preparation for the coming offensive.

Germany was well aware that, whilst Britain and France were fatigued, American forces were growing stronger in France by the day. The USA had declared war upon Germany in April 1917 but declined to bolster weakened Allied divisions in a piecemeal fashion. Under General Pershing, America decided to fight as an independent force and would not be pressurized into action until they had sufficient numbers of trained troops to achieve that ambition. Thousands of fit, young Americans began arriving each month.

It could only be a matter of time before the Allied armies were sufficiently strong to finally crush the German defences and drive them back. And perhaps even invade their beloved homeland. They decided to strike and hopefully drive a wedge between the British and French armies. It had been politically decided to keep back over one million new British soldiers from the fighting and so, in March 1918, we were not as strong as would have been desired. The French armies were still recovering from mass mutiny in 1917 – although somehow the Germans seemed unaware of this. New German tactics were tried and these, combined with surprise, massive artillery bombardments, foggy weather (which prevented aerial observation) and huge concentrations of soldiers, enabled the Germans to break through our lines in several places.

There were five main attacks in Operation Kaiserschlacht (the Kaiser's Battle). They began on 21 March 1918 with the Michael Offensive against a weak British 5th Army, east of the old Somme battlefields. The British retreated, losing much ground, material and men. Other attacks followed from April to July, in areas ranging from the British areas south of Ypres to the French Marne sectors. The Germans kept up the pressure until August 1918 when, in essence, their attack 'ran out of steam'.

Deep inside enemy territory the German armies were low on supplies and exhausted from fighting an ever-stiffening British and French defence.

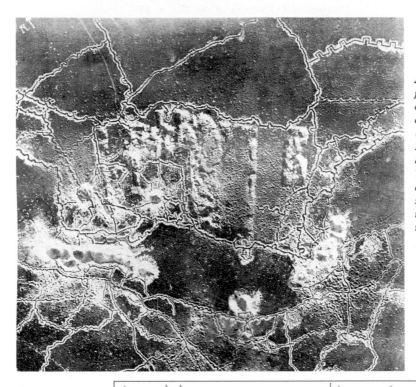

Aerial photograph of area east of Vermelles (Map 36C NW3 G11 and 12). The trench castellations show clearly in the top right.

Official interpretation of features in aerial photograph 36C G11 and 12.

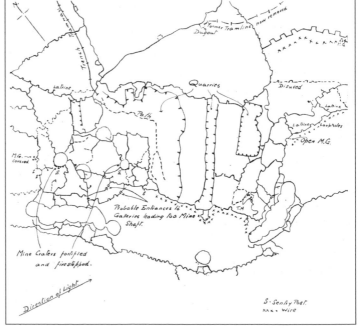

The naval blockade on Germany was biting and her population undernourished. Although higher quality food was diverted to the army it was not really sufficient or very exciting. Ersatz, meaning substitute, was the norm. For example, coffee was synthetic. It was made from ground acorns and other nuts. Bread was adulterated with sawdust to eke out the meagre grain supplies. Life was not luxurious for the German soldier. Even his boots were of inferior quality as leather was scarce. Indeed that is the reason why so many photographs of dead Allied soldiers show them without boots. They were 'salvaged' by their killers. When the German conquerors came across British supply dumps they could not

THE DUD SHELL—OR THE FUSE-TOP COLLECTOR
" Give it a good 'ard 'un, Bert; you can generally 'ear 'em fizzing a bit first if they are a-goin' to explode."

A sardonic but apt cartoon by Bairnsfather. Many soldiers were killed tinkering with munitions.

believe their eyes. They were crammed with the luxuries of life such as real food, real coffee, real soap, wool blankets, proper clothes and alcohol. They were totally demoralized by the extent of the British supplies, much of which came from America. In consequence very many German soldiers literally took 'time out' to loot and gorge and get drunk.

With the onslaught finally halted just outside the vital town of Amiens in August 1918 the Allied steamroller, led by Britain and her Commonwealth Allies, commenced. It was open warfare at last. Communications had improved. New tactics, aided by tanks and masses of aircraft, to attack German positions and troop concentrations, wreaked havoc. During that time various vicious and vital actions were also fought by French and American Divisions with the help of their airmen. The famous 'last 100 days' of the war were under way and the German armies were finally beaten into submission and the Armistice.

Other Theatres Involving British Forces

China: Tsing-Tau

The Germans had a naval base at Tsing-Tau in north China. It was home to Vice-Admiral Graf von Spee's German East Asiatic Squadron that had set sail to peacefully visit far-flung parts of empire in June 1914. With war declared, it was subsequently to wreak havoc in the Pacific before being finally destroyed itself at the Falklands in December 1914. As the German naval base was a threat it was decided to mount a joint amphibious assault on it in conjunction with Japanese forces. After a naval bombardment the forces landed unopposed eighteen miles from Tsing-Tau on 23 September and moved, with much difficulty, into position. Following artillery bombardments to break the siege, and after fierce fighting, the German garrison surrendered on 7 November 1914.

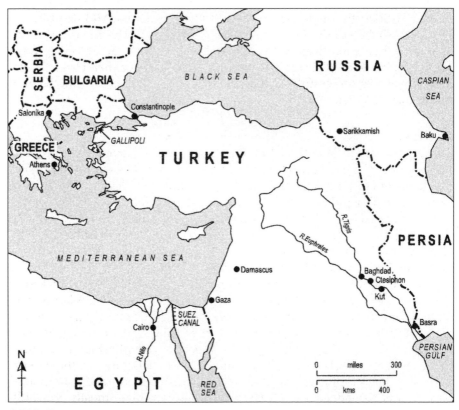

Middle East. Sue Rowland

Middle East – Introduction:

The various theatres of war, which grew in the Middle East, developed from a simple concept. In late November 1914 an idea was mooted by Churchill to the War Council that involvement in the region would serve several purposes. If the Dardanelles could be forced by the navy, at that time not heavily engaged elsewhere, then Constantinople might well be seized or at least dominated. That would demoralize the Turks, following a declaration of war against them on 5 November 1914. It might persuade other states in the region towards the Allied cause. There was always a possibility that Turkey might capitulate or even join the Allies – after all, it was not clear in August 1914 which way she would lean. That would have made defending the vital Suez Canal very much easier. Another major consideration was that a successful operation, resulting in free passage through the Dardanelles to the Black Sea, would open up an all-seasons route to Russia for the transportation of weapons and materials; she was already in desperate need of these. Britain also had to guard its oil supplies from the Middle East.

As we shall see, the Dardanelles was not forced. The invasion of the Gallipoli Peninsula was a failure and the actions at Salonica were unproductive. Mesopotamia was not initially a success either. However the Suez Canal was successfully defended and the Egyptian campaign the only real accomplishment.

Gallipoli

Those who served in both Gallipoli and in France regarded the former as many times worse. Apart from the normal privations of warfare against a relentless enemy, the climatic conditions were merciless to the British, Commonwealth and French troops who landed there.

Flies covered everything in sight, including each mouthful of food, with the result that dysentery was prevalent. Most men were subject to the 'Turkey Trot' but stayed at their posts until (almost) too weak to walk to the latrine unaided. Some fell into the latrine and drowned there.

This theatre of war really commenced on 19 February 1915 with a joint British and French naval bombardment of Turkish forts. The plan was to force a way through the straits by sheer power of arms by naval forces alone. It was not successful and several ships were sunk or damaged, with considerable loss of life. During the campaign six battleships and many other smaller vessels were lost, with over 600 perishing in the French battleship *Bouvet* alone. Almost as many British sailors died when HMS *Goliath* was torpedoed on 13 May. Seaborne landings, mostly violently

Table 1. Total military deaths at Gallipoli (killed in action, died of wounds and died of other causes)	
British Army	29,134
Royal Naval Division	2,489
Australian Forces	8,709
New Zealand Forces	2,721
Newfoundland Regiment	49
Indian native troops	1,358
French Army (estimated)	10,000
Turkish Army (estimated)	more than 60,000

opposed, were undertaken by British, French, Newfoundland, Indian, Australian and New Zealand troops.

Despite great heroism and considerable loss of life, it was not possible to conquer the peninsula and advance north, as had been planned, to open a viable second front against Turkey and the Central Powers. Eventually most troops were evacuated in December 1915, with the remainder leaving the Cape Helles zone on 8 January 1916. The campaign was finally abandoned.

Although the loss of life by the ANZAC (Australia New Zealand Army Corps) was not as great as the British or French, proportionate to their small populations, it was seen as catastrophic. To commemorate their war dead a public holiday on 25 April in both countries marks the day of the landing of their forces at Anzac Cove on the west of the Gallipoli Peninsula.

Whereas extraordinary figures for dead and injured in this campaign are sometimes suggested, the approximate numbers, using official sources where possible, are shown here. Unfortunately those official sources tend to disagree with each other – especially for British casualties. Most sources give the number of British officers and men who died at around 22,000. Investigation by Gallipoli Association members produces very different figures and it is their well-researched total that is quoted here for the British Army. The differences could be accounted for by the subsequent deaths of those who left the area sick or wounded. Over 410,000 British and Commonwealth military personnel took part in the operation. There were in addition over 80,000 French soldiers and thousands of British and French sailors. Disease was rife during the campaign and nearly half those sent were affected by it, with almost 2,000 dying from non-battle causes. Well over one thousand sailors were killed or drowned. When considering the deaths we must remember that more than twice these numbers were seriously wounded.

Italy

Having at last been persuaded, by promises of territories when victorious, to join the Entente, Italy at last declared war on Austria-Hungary on 23 May 1915. Under Generalissimo Luigi Cadorna the Italians lost a great many men in fruitless frontal assaults against well-defended, yet numerically inferior, Austro-Hungarian positions in an extremely difficult terrain for fighting. Little ground was gained and a stalemate situation ensued with neither side gaining the advantage.

The overall objective of the Italians was the strategic port of Trieste but war raged from the high Tyrol to the shores of the River Isonzo, where altogether twelve punishing battles were fought between June 1915 and November 1917. Following the Italian declaration of war on Germany on 27 August 1916, elite mountain troops, some led by then acting Major (later Field Marshal) Erwin Rommel, took to the offensive and forced mass retreats and surrenders by the Italians.

To bolster its ally, Britain and France each sent sizeable expeditionary forces in late 1917. Their responsibility moved from a supporting role to fierce fighting, in rather mountainous terrains in the Piave and adjacent regions, not previously experienced by the British during the war. In excess of 80,000 British combat troops served, and well over 1,000 British officers and men died on the Italian front. American troops were also deployed in this region but saw very little action.

Mesopotamia

This is the area, formerly part of the Ottoman Empire, now known as Iraq. Following a naval bombardment and landing a small force, a joint Anglo-Indian 'Force D' invaded, almost unopposed, in November 1914. With war against Turkey declared on 2 November 1914, its purpose was to 'show the flag', ostensibly protect vital oil installations, and safeguard the Shatt-al-Arab waterway. That was the name given to the united streams of the Tigris and Euphrates rivers flowing into the Persian Gulf below Basra. The ease of the operation in the early days, which included the taking of Basra as forward base, lulled Force D into overconfidence in its own powers. The Turkish army, a formidable power to be reckoned with, was totally underestimated. Turkish soldiers had launched inconclusive offensives and raids against oil pipelines but had done nothing, so far, to unduly worry the Anglo-Indian force.

A mission was despatched to conquer Baghdad some 400km to the north. It was launched with inadequate intelligence and insufficient resources. After getting to within 40km of its target, the column was attacked by some 20,000 well-armed and determined Turks and lost heavily in the engagement. Retreat to the town of Kut-al-Amara, lying inside a large loop of the River Tigris, followed. Force D was besieged there for nearly five months, losing many men through disease and even starvation, as the several attempts to rescue them by land and by river failed. Even airdrops of food and ammunition were attempted.

With summer temperatures regularly exceeding 50 degrees Celsius, it would be a further year before Baghdad fell. Eventually over 250,000 Allied soldiers were deployed against a Turkish force one-fifth their size. But disease and the hostile terrain favoured the enemy. Operations, with limited success, in the region continued right up to the armistice with Turkey on 30 October 1918.

Egypt and Palestine

Predominant in this region was the Suez Canal – a vital artery through which essential war supplies of men and materials, including food and oil, reached the Allies from the Middle East, India and the Far East. It had to be defended at all costs from the hostile Turkish forces, bolstered by some German units and officers, already ensconced in the area. Muslim Egypt was heavily influenced by the Ottoman Empire, while to the east lay vast tracts of Turkish territory. The many disparate Arab factions in the Middle East were gradually united in their cause against the historical conqueror of their lands. Encouraged by Britain, especially Colonel T E Lawrence, they eventually engaged the Turks in guerrilla warfare. Egypt became the headquarters of the Mediterranean Expeditionary Force. However, its divisions were regarded by London as a strategic reserve for other theatres of war if necessary, besides defending the local area.

Britain and her allies, most notably India, Australia and New Zealand and with help from the French, conducted a very successful campaign. Turkish attacks against the canal were thwarted. The terrain was ideally suited to cavalry operations (both horse and camel) and aircraft played their part in reconnaissance and ground-attack. Operations to press north towards Syria initially met with limited success. Eventually, aided by reinforcements of men and supplies, and with good leadership, the Allies

Privately made identity discs. Those from Salonica and Baghdad illustrate boredom.

advanced in September 1918 to take Aleppo, not far from the Turkish border itself. Fighting ceased, as it did in Mesopotamia, with the armistice with Turkey on 30 October 1918.

Macedonia (Salonica)

Macedonia was an area of land through which ran a railway line linking the strategically important Greek port of Salonica on the Aegean Sea with Belgrade, capital of Serbia. When Bulgaria joined the Central Powers in September 1915, the Allies, at the invitation of the Greek government, landed troops at Salonica with the idea of supporting Serbia. Moving slowly north, they arrived too late to aid the Serbs, and the poorly equipped Anglo-French force retreated to a defensive position around the port of Salonica. They were surrounded on the landward side by large contingents of Bulgarian and German soldiers and, despite minor actions, effectively remained trapped in their enclave from November 1915 until September 1918. Much intrigue ensued involving the Greeks and it was not always clear whose side they were really on. Reinforced by fresh British, French and Serbian troops by sea, breakout was finally achieved and Bulgaria invaded. It was hardly a victory, for by then the German stiffening had been withdrawn to the Western Front and Bulgaria offered little resistance. Altogether over one million Allied soldiers were deployed in the area at one time or other and perhaps half fell victim to malaria and other diseases in this unhealthy place. The soldiers could arguably have been better deployed elsewhere and Macedonia had the unenviable reputation of being 'Germany's biggest internment camp'.

Africa

Germany had colonies in East Africa, South West Africa, the Cameroons and Togoland. The small German garrisons in all but East Africa (essentially present-day Tanzania) surrendered in 1914 or 1915. Conversely, the small East African forces under Colonel (later General) von Lettow-Vorbeck fought a successful guerrilla campaign against numerically superior British, Indian and African forces. The German territory, despite being blockaded to cut off supplies, kept going by using captured weapons and ammunition and husbanding its own resources. Intermittent skirmishes ranged over a vast area of eastern Africa and involved British East Africa (Kenya and Uganda), Northern Rhodesia (Zambia), Belgian Congo and Mozambique. The tactics used by von Lettow-Vorbeck tied down the British Empire forces for the whole war. Most of the casualties on both sides were the result of disease rather than enemy action, although hundreds were nevertheless killed in action. An attempt to resupply von Lettow-Vorbeck by Zeppelin from a base in Bulgaria failed after the airship turned back following false reports that he had surrendered. In fact, unaware that the war was eventually over, he did not surrender until 25 November 1918.

Russia

At the time of the Great War, Russia was a highly complex nation that warrants extensive study. The British involvement with it was mainly confined to sending massive aid in war materials. They did however get embroiled in fighting in mainland Russia, partly to protect their own interests in the Artic and partly to support the White Armies against the Communist Red Army. Britain was not alone. France, the United States of America and Japan also sent soldiers. They were in actions across much of Russia, ranging from Archangel in the north, to Vladivostok in the east of that vast nation. The allies slowly lost ground against the Red Army and they finally withdrew on 10 October 1919.

Other Areas Not Involving British Forces

As well as the areas involving British and Empire forces there was extensive warfare in Eastern Europe. Although it principally concerned Germany with Austria-Hungary fighting Russia and Serbia, several other nations, such as Romania and Bulgaria, were involved. The battles covered huge areas, much of it in Poland and East Prussia, and a great many lives were lost. Although not as well covered by English-language books as the Western Front, there are several that deal adequately with this aspect of the Great War.

Following the Armistice there was continued unrest and fighting in parts of the Middle East. For example, Turkey was in turmoil and in conflict with Greece until October 1922, which involved mass population exchanges. The RAF was used to police the region and sometimes ground troops were involved as well in maintaining law and order in Iraq and Persia for many years after the war.

Royal Navy

Whereas most soldiers engaged in fighting were able, albeit perhaps unwillingly, to see what was going on, few in the Royal Navy witnessed the actions their ships fought. Most were entombed within the steel cladding of their pitching warship, doing their job amid noise and smoke, but unable to see beyond their action station. Certain officers and lookouts were often the only ones to actually see an enemy vessel – and then usually only at several miles distance. Many sailors were never in action. Some remained in shore stations, affectionately called concrete battleships, or spent the war swinging around the anchor in harbour. Others were sent, as part of the Royal Naval Division, to fight alongside the army ashore.

From the very beginning of the war the Royal Navy blockaded Germany. It was not a close blockade but maintained at a distance to stop and capture or sink merchant vessels and so slowly starve Germany. The Imperial German Navy was largely impotent and unable to defend its merchantmen whereas the Royal Navy, together with the ships of our allies, literally ruled the waves. This blockade contributed considerably to the downfall of Germany.

Various famous actions were fought about which much has been written over the decades and it is not necessary to repeat the details here. The words

The mighty battleship was to be outclassed by the invisible submarine.

Heligoland Bight, Dogger Bank, Coronel, Jutland and actions such as that at Zeebrugge, are on the lips of everyone who has read about the war at sea. Ships put to sea and shore batteries engaged German ships bombarding northeast coastal towns. Cruisers patrolled the oceans, keeping Allied shipping lanes free from German raiders. Most big ship actions were indecisive and yet many lives were lost. The vast majority of casualties at sea, in all branches of shipping, remain at sea. It is their grave.

During the First World War the battleship theoretically reigned supreme. Improvements in guns, gunnery, protective armour and speed were made all the time. The fleets were huge and the cost of producing and maintaining them immense. They required colossal manpower and yet the most powerful elements of all fleets, those massive battleships, saw relatively little action. In truth it was submarines on both sides that decided the course of the war at sea. Both sides sank a huge tonnage of shipping with much loss of life.

One of the most controversial actions of the Great War was the sinking of RMS *Lusitania* on 7 May 1915, which resulted in 1,198 deaths. It was sunk by U-20, one of a fleet of submarines that altogether sank nearly 13 million tons of Allied shipping. This resulted in severe shortages of supplies for Britain. Of over 350 submarines built, the Imperial German Navy lost over 200 during the course of the war. By comparison, of the total British submarine fleet of over 200 boats – some of which were obsolete, 54 were lost. Submarines are traditionally referred to as 'boats' – not ships! The German name for a submarine was 'unterseeboot', or U-boot (U-boat) for short.

Another weapon of naval warfare employed by both sides was the sea mine. It was tethered to a weight on the seabed and floated a few feet below the surface. It was detonated by direct impact with a passing ship or submarine. Various

The badge of the Mine Clearance Service.

areas of the seas around Britain and the continental shelf were mined to prevent unauthorized access by each side. Generally one's own minefields were well charted with safe passages noted but mines often broke free from their moorings and drifted away from their planned positions. It was a mine that sank HMS *Hampshire* en route to Russia on 5 June 1916. Almost everybody on board was lost including Field Marshal Kitchener. Another famous incident was when Turkish mines guarding the Dardanelles stopped it being forced by British and French fleets in March 1915. Fleets of small ships were eventually equipped to counter the mine threat and were very successful, but many mines remain in the seas to this day – a legacy of the Great War.

Merchant Navy

These were the brave men who fought not only the enemy but also the elements, in ships not always of the highest quality. If armed at all it was with a few surplus or obsolete guns, manned, usually, by Royal Navy personnel. Without the merchant fleets, and also the fishing fleets, Britain would have starved. It was not self-sufficient in food or war materials and needed to import a great deal. Before the days of the convoy system merchantmen sailed alone, and were easy prey to surface raiders and submarines that attacked them at will. With convoys, whereby a large number of merchant ships were grouped together and protected by escorting warships, the dangers receded but never passed. It was still easy for a torpedo to be aimed at a ship unseen from beneath the waves. Some 3,305 British merchant ships were sunk during the Great War, with more than 17,000 officers and sailors being killed. Most have no known grave and are commemorated on a special memorial at Tower Hill in London.

The Air Services (RFC, RNAS and RAF)

Although their stores and main personnel travelled to France by ship, most aircraft of the original Royal Flying Corps contingent of just four squadrons took to the air and flew across the Channel. The first to arrive did so on 12 August 1914. Their initial job was reconnaissance to determine the location of the German invaders. The eye in the sky had arrived. On 22 August the first contact was made and a German column identified. The aircraft was unfortunately shot down by ground fire and became the first ever to be lost due to enemy action. See Chapter 10 for details.

From that small beginning the Corps expanded rapidly. Because of the limitations of early aircraft no fixed armaments were carried and only lightweight officers were accepted as pilots. As their primary role was reconnaissance, it ideally suited former cavalry officers used to the 'light-touch' required to control horses and essential to fly the delicate flying machines of 1914. Overall about one-third of deaths among flyers were caused by accidents.

Once more powerful machines were developed each side tried to deprive the other of air space. After five confirmed aircraft 'kills' (balloons counted as a half-kill) a pilot was known as an 'ace'. Despite the highly publicized exploits of those aces, on both sides, they had little real effect upon the war.

Spotting the fall of shots for the artillery became commonplace. Contact with the ground was usually one way only. Initially, messages placed inside weighted streamers were thrown out. Later primitive transmitting radios were used.

First the Royal Naval Air Service, then the Royal Flying Corps and later the Royal Air Force deployed large numbers of fixed kite balloons for observation over enemy lines. They were usually either the Drachen or the French Caquot types. Beneath each canopy was slung a wickerwork basket that held two observers, typically an officer and an NCO. The men were attached, whilst airborne, to prepacked parachutes that were contained in inverted cones attached to the outside of the basket. Initially only home-made harnesses were available. In an emergency the act of jumping from

Launching a kite balloon.

the basket pulled the parachute free from its container and deployed it and over 400 lives were thus saved during the war. Although defended by anti-aircraft guns sited on the ground, most often the observers went aloft unarmed in the fond hope that enemy aircraft would only shoot at the balloon and not at its crew. The balloons were tethered to a tender (lorry) by a cable that was unwound to allow the balloon to ascend to above 6,000 feet (1,800m) altitude. It could be rapidly rewound on a drum mechanism if attacked. Communication with the ground was by telephone along a separate cable to that supporting the hydrogen-filled balloon. To distinguish their status qualified observers wore a special single winged badge with the letter 'O' attached.

Bombing of strategic targets, such as Zeppelin sheds and railway junctions, was undertaken with limited success, due to the primitive methods of aiming the bomb. Tactics to bomb and strafe (machine gun) troops on the ground were slowly improved and caused much damage and consternation, especially in the latter part of the war.

Ships were escorted, usually by the Royal Naval Air Service, and that arm also undertook anti-submarine searches and attacks. For these missions

Bristol Fighter of the Royal Flying Corps, 1917.

the RNAS frequently flew highly manoeuvrable airships of various designs.

Squadrons of aircraft were kept in Britain to protect us from air raids by Zeppelins and German bombers. Attempts failed to shoot down any airship, some of which bombed with apparent immunity from heights of up to 19,000 feet, until Lieutenant Leefe Robinson shot one down on 3 September 1916 over Cuffley in Essex. It was technically not a Zeppelin but a wood-framed Schutte-Lanz airship. Of whatever design, all the hydrogen-filled hulls were very vulnerable to the new incendiary bullets and airship raids soon ceased.

Late in the war long-range bombing was undertaken. Various bombs, culminating in the 1,650lb (750kg) heavy bomb carried by the Hanley Page O/400 late in 1918, were carried to cities in western Germany in an attempt to interrupt armament production. Although judged to be of military importance, the success of those air raids was minimal.

As an independent air force the Royal Air Force was formed on 1 April 1918. It encompassed the Royal Flying Corps and the Royal Naval Air Service and had a separate command structure from the military and navy. From a tiny beginning, by the time of the Armistice the RAF possessed, albeit not all in good order, many thousands of flying machines of one kind or other. Later, the navy re-established its own airborne branch and became separate again in 1937.

Aircraft carriers as such did not play much of a role in the Great War. It is true that several ships were converted as seaplane launchers – indeed, one was used to spot for the capital ships guns in the Dardanelles. In addition many larger warships carried seaplanes. Some could be launched from the parent ship, being flown off temporary platforms built over forward gun barrels. Others were lowered over the side to take off. All were recovered by crane after landing at sea. It was not until after the war that the modern conception of an aircraft carrier emerged.

Attacks on Britain

Most, but not all, of the German airmen who died and were buried in the UK were exhumed and are now interred at the German War Cemetery at Cannock Chase, in Staffordshire.

Table 2. Attacks on Britain			
Type	Number of raids	Killed	Injured
Airship raids	48	556	1,357
Aeroplane raids	59	857	2,050
Coastal bombardments	12	157	634

Armistice Details

The Armistice (a ceasefire only – not a peace agreement) was agreed at 5am on 11 November 1918 in a railway carriage in the Forest of Compiègne and came into effect at 11am, Paris time. It was signalled to units thus:

Hostilities will cease at 11.00 on November 11th. Troops will stand fast on the line reached at that hour which will be reported by wire to GHQ. Defence precautions will be maintained. There will be no intercourse of any description with the enemy until receipt of instructions from GHQ. Further instructions will follow.

The principal signatories of the Armistice were Marshal Foch for the Allies, and Matthias Erzberger, the German representative. That effectively brought the Great War to an end in most of Europe. There were several armistices to end fighting between the various belligerents and not all were adhered to. For example, fighting resumed between the Central Powers and Russia after an earlier ceasefire in December 1917 and much Russian territory was (temporarily) lost. Most combat ceased towards the end of 1918 but continued in parts of Russia, the Middle East and between Greece and Turkey. Parts of Germany were occupied by Britain, France and America for several years, which caused much resentment.

The Aftermath

Among the many tragedies of the Great War were the hundreds of thousands of eligible young women destined to forever remain single. Britain, before the war, already had a surplus of over half a million more women than men. With so many young men killed or crippled for life, well over a million women were doomed to never marry – the one thing that, above all else, most women of that generation aspired to. Fortunately nature seems to have stepped in and the post-war birth rate shot up to restore most of our lost youth during the next two decades. A not dissimilar situation existed in France and Germany, and indeed in every other country, where the scythe of war had cut down so many young men.

Unemployment hit Britain soon after the war and jobs became scarce. The vast quantities of war materials were no longer required and the country's industry rapidly returned to peacetime production. During the war around one million women took over jobs traditionally done by men. When the boys came home they were not anxious to return to their earlier drab and poorly paid existence. They expected better. In 1929 the Wall Street crash brought unemployment and misery to many of those who had found work. For those still out of work it made life harder still. It was not a happy time for the men who had expected to return home to a grateful government and a land fit for heroes. Much discontentment prevailed, not just in Britain, but around the world. It became the excuse for extreme government on both sides of the political divide and was to culminate in another world war.

Chapter 2

THE ARMY

Structure of the British Army in 1914

By 1914 the soldiery of the army was quite complex and comprised Regular, Reserve and Territorial Force officers and other ranks. Men in the Regular Army usually enlisted for twelve years. They most often served about seven years with the Colours (that is, as 'armed' soldiers in uniform) followed by five years in one or more classes of Reserve.

It was possible for the ratio of Regular and Reserve Service to vary considerably but the man was not totally free from military jurisdiction for the full twelve years. There were different categories and subcategories of Army Reserve Service depending upon the conditions of the soldiers' release from Regular Service. When war was declared the entire British Army was comprised of 247,482 Regular officers and men, 316,094 Territorials and 228,120 conventional Reservists that included 3,000 ex-Regular officers on reserve. The above figures include staff and other non-effective appointments not available for deployment to theatres of war. By November 1918 the overall total then serving had risen to nearly three and a half million.

In 1908 the Militia (an earlier type of territorial army that had evolved in a rather

Typical British Tommy in 1914. A soldier of 4th Middlesex Regt near Mons.

disjointed way over hundreds of years) was partially disbanded and the remainder formed sections of the Special Reserve and Territorial Force. The Special Reserve was part of the first class of the Army Reserve. It included cavalry, corps troops and infantry – of which there were seventy-four Special Reserve battalions and twenty-seven Extra Special Reserve battalions. Former regular soldiers could also join the Special Reserve and after retraining return to civilian life, subject to recall in an emergency. The conditions for service in all reserve units were numerous and are detailed in the *Manual of Military Law 1914*.

Infantry reservists were allocated to certain battalions of their regiment but not physically attached to those battalions unless called up. Those reserve battalions were, in peacetime, the Depot or recruiting battalions and often numbered three in the regimental order. Each such battalion was staffed by around 100 regular officers and men for recruiting and training purposes. In peacetime, the newly trained soldier would not have stayed with the Depot but would have been posted to one of the regular battalions (generally the first or second battalions). Any surplus reservists on call-up not required to reinforce the regular battalions would be assigned as Special Reservists to the reserve (Depot) battalion. There, they would train recruits or be reassigned to the regular battalions when vacancies (casualties) occurred. Some went as instructors to the New Armies. They also took over the duties of regular garrisons at home. In 1914 there were 101 Reserve and Extra Reserve infantry (but not guards) battalions.

The National Reserve consisted of former trained servicemen who were no longer in any other type of reserve unit. They could elect, subject to conditions, to register to serve in an emergency. They were generally older men and were paid an annual grant depending upon which category they joined.

The Territorial Force was extensive and comprised infantry, artillery, engineer, transport, medical and veterinary units. It was originally intended for home defence. Men enlisted initially for four years and could re-engage subject to certain conditions. Preliminary training was given and then men were required to attend a number of drills and annual training camps. They were subject to call-up to full-time service in an emergency (embodiment) but, unlike the Special Reserve, were not obliged to serve overseas; they could however volunteer to do so.

Reservists were paid to compensate them for training times and continuing commitment. Officers as well as men served in all reserve units and were subject to Military Law.

It was technically possible for regular soldiers and reservists to complete their full period of commitment during a crisis – or even during a war. They were then discharged and free to leave. But when compulsory service came into force they could be conscripted back into the army – assuming they had not already volunteered to stay on!

Various other reserve classes were created during the war to encompass men who could be called up but were temporarily, at least, more valuably engaged in their civilian occupation. Those classes were P, T and W and it depended upon the man's job and medical category as to which he was allocated. It was not uncommon for a man to serve in the field, be transferred out of the army to a reserve class and then be recalled to the Colours later.

When the war was over most men were not immediately given their complete freedom but were transferred to Class Z Reserve on demobilization. That meant they could be recalled should an emergency arise – such as a resumption of hostilities by Germany. They were not finally released until 31 March 1920.

All figures quoted in the following sections are for the prescribed war establishment and assume full strength. It must be realized that all units were rarely at full strength.

Ole Bill Bus, once used to transport troops, carrying veterans in London.

Army Command

All members of the armed forces swore allegiance to the King. On his behalf the Army was administered by the Army Council. That in turn was chaired by the Secretary of State for War, as minister responsible for the War Office. The council was comprised of both military and civilian members. Its military adviser was the Chief of the Imperial General Staff (CIGS).

Various forces were set up during the war. They came under the jurisdiction of a command structure, which was known as either General Headquarters (GHQ) or sometimes Headquarters (HQ) – depending on the rank or seniority of the general in local command. At various times during the war the following GHQ were established:

Home Forces
British Expeditionary Force (BEF) France and Flanders and later Italy
Egyptian Expeditionary Force (EEF)
Mediterranean Expeditionary Force (MEF)
Mesopotamia
British Salonica Army
East Africa

Going to War

In early August 1914 the British Expeditionary Force sailed for France. It comprised two Army Corps consisting of four infantry divisions. (A third corps was held back by Kitchener for home defence.) There were also two cavalry divisions – a grand total of 81,000 officers and men. Reinforcements in the shape of reservists, regular soldiers returning from overseas stations, Indian soldiers and territorials, followed rapidly. By mid-December 1914 the BEF numbered 269,711 officers and men. To that number must be added over 22,500 officers and men who had already been killed by December, plus tens of thousands more wounded. By November 1918 those original two Army Corps had expanded somewhat as can be seen in Table 3.

During the course of the war, divisions frequently moved between Army Corps and the composition of all echelons changed to suit the demands of High Command. The *Orders of Battle* (see Bibliography) chronicles these changes.

Table 3. Higher formations of the British Expeditionary Force

August 1914

Commander in Chief	Field Marshal Sir John French.
I Army Corps	Lieutenant-General Sir Douglas Haig, 1st and 2nd Divisions.
II Army Corps	General Sir Horace Smith-Dorrien, 3rd and 5th Divisions.
III Army Corps	Major General William Pulteney, 4th and 6th Divisions. (Formed in France, 31 August 1914)

November 1918

Commander in Chief	Field Marshal Sir Douglas Haig.
First Army	General Sir Henry Horne.
VII Army Corps	Major-General Sir Robert Whigham (reserve June 1918).
VIII Army Corps	Lieutenant-General Sir Aylmer Hunter-Weston, 8th, 12th (Eastern), 49th (West Riding) and 52nd (Lowland) Divisions.
XXII Army Corps	Lieutenant-General Sir Alexander Godley, 4th, 11th (Northern), 51st (Highland), 56th (London) and 63rd (Royal Naval) Division.
Canadian Army Corps	Lieutenant-General Sir Arthur Currie, 1st, 2nd, 3rd and 4th Canadian Divisions.
Second Army	General Sir Herbert Plumer.
II Army Corps	Lieutenant-General Sir Claud Jacob, 9th (Scottish) and 34th Divisions.
X Army Corps	Lieutenant-General Reginald Stephens, 29th and 30th Divisions.
XV Army Corps	Lieutenant-General Sir Henry de Beauvoir De Lisle, 14th (Light), 36th (Ulster) and 40th Divisions.
XIX Army Corps	Lieutenant-General Sir Herbert Watts, 31st, 35th and 41st Divisions.
Third Army	General Hon. Sir Julian Byng.
IV Army Corps	Lieutenant-General Sir George Harper, 5th, 37th, 42nd (East Lancashire) and the New Zealand Divisions.

V Army Corps	Lieutenant-General Cameron Shute, 17th (Northern), 21st, 33rd and 38th (Welsh) Divisions.
VI Army Corps	Lieutenant-General Sir James Haldane, Guards, 2nd, 3rd and 62nd (West Riding) Divisions.
XVII Army Corps	Lieutenant-General Sir Charles Fergusson, Bt., 19th (Western), 20th (Light), 24th and 61st (South Midland Divisions).
Fourth Army	General Sir Henry Rawlinson, Bt.
IX Army Corps	Lieutenant-General Sir William Braithwaite, 1st, 6th, 32nd and 46th (North Midland) Divisions.
XIII Army Corps	Lieutenant-General Sir Thomas Morland, 18th (Eastern), 25th, 50th (Northumbrian and 66th Divisions.
Australian Army Corps	Lieutenant-General Sir John Monash, 1st, 2nd, 3rd, 4th and 5th Australian Divisions.
Fifth Army	General Sir William Birdwood.
I Army Corps	Lieutenant-General Sir Arthur Holland, 15th (Scottish), 16th (Irish) and 58th (London) Divisions.
II Army Corps	Lieutenant-General Sir Richard Butler, 55th (West Lancashire) and 74th (Yeomanry) Divisions.
XI Army Corps	Lieutenant-General Sir Richard Haking, 47th (London), 57th and 59th Divisions.
Portuguese Corps	General Garcia Rosado, 1st and 2nd Portuguese Divisions.

Note: There were additionally cavalry divisions and others in lines of communication.

Enlistment

Volunteers

Field Marshal Lord Kitchener, as Minister of State for War, persuaded the Cabinet that the war against Germany would not be quickly or easily won. He considered it would take at least three years to defeat the highly efficient and well-equipped German Armies. Kitchener therefore encouraged mass recruitment and the country responded to the call.

The men who flocked to the Colours were all volunteers and they were largely assigned to new formations. These were created specifically to cater for the rapid enlargement of the army necessitated by the war. Some men intentionally joined the Territorial Force but this was not encouraged. Kitchener decided it was best to build entirely new armies rather than expand the existing one. He was of the opinion it would be a long war, which could only be won by large, well-organized and well-trained forces. The existing army structure was totally inadequate to allow for massive expansion. Many new divisions were required to accommodate the numbers of men deemed necessary to win the war. Kitchener did not consider the territorials were sufficiently highly trained to bolster the regulars and was not sure they would volunteer for overseas service in sufficient

The famous poster depicting the accusing finger of Field Marshal Kitchener.

numbers. In the event their training proceeded apace and most agreed to fight overseas – many serving with great distinction.

Those responding to the 'call' could largely choose their regiment and were subject, in theory at least, to the same physical fitness and age constraints that applied to the regular army. For it was indeed the regular army they were joining, even if not entirely on the same terms. They mostly signed up for three years or the duration of the war. The idea was that these men would be trained and then sent into battle as complete units. Some were however required as soon as possible to fill gaps in the ranks of existing battalions. Eventually five New Armies were to be created and, popularly known as Kitchener's Army, were numbered from K1 to K5. These armies mostly contained six divisions (K5 had seven), each of twelve battalions.

Officers who had left the army years before were 'dug out' of retirement and many old soldiers re-enlisted and were promoted to train new recruits. Some were better than others at their new tasks. Both officers and NCOs who had been wounded in France were eagerly sought after on their recovery for the New Armies. Recent experience was desperately needed.

The tide-swell of men coming forward voluntarily gradually diminished and to maintain the flow other measures were necessary. Upper age limits were increased but that did not produce enough men. It was decided to see how many men were theoretically available for the armed forces. A census was conducted under the National Registration Act of 1915 to establish the numbers, ages and trades of the male population.

Enlistment expanded with the introduction of conscription and the traditional regimental system became overloaded. From September 1916, Training Reserve Brigades comprising three, four or five Reserve Battalions were formed. Further changes from May 1917 resulted in Graduated and Young Soldier Battalions being formed. Young Soldier battalions recruited men aged 18 and after basic training these soldiers were transferred to Graduated Battalions. They were then ready for home service and, if required, for overseas service. The battalions were eventually attached to existing regiments and their deployment can be traced in the *Order of Battle of Divisions* and other sources.

One effect of the rush to volunteer was that, once in, it was difficult to get out again. Captains of industry often pleaded in vain for the release of men whose expertise was vital to the war effort at home and currently being 'wasted' in the trenches.

Derby Scheme

In October 1915 Lord Derby was appointed Director General of Recruiting. He introduced a system, which became known as the 'Derby Scheme', whereby males between 18 and 40 were asked to either enlist or register for call-up if required. They were told that the chance to volunteer and thus have some choice of regiment etc. was soon to end. Compulsion loomed! Those on the register were classified, depending upon age and marital status, as ready for enlistment when required. There were many exemptions from potential call-up, for example, because of special job skills. The process produced well over two million actual and potential recruits but many did not register before the scheme closed on 15 December 1915 and so the next step was taken. Often those on the register were not actually attested for many months.

Conscription

The Military Service Act, which came into effect from 2 March 1916, was extended and modified in May 1916 to include married men, and made enlistment into the armed forces compulsory. Men could no longer choose their regiment etc. Again there were many exemptions and various tribunals heard appeals against service. These appeals were generally reported in the local press for all to see the excuses offered. If exemption was granted it was often conditional. For example, if the man left a reserved occupation he was immediately liable for service. Other authorities, such as government departments, could approve exemption from call-up. When a notice of call-up was issued, usually with a railway warrant for free travel, the recipient had to report to a specific recruiting office at the time stipulated – usually about two weeks later. By April 1918 age limits were again extended – this time to those between 18 and 50.

Officers

When the war started so many new officers were required that the supply could not equal the demand. Potential reserves of officers were soon exhausted. Officers Training Corps attached to universities, public schools and certain similar establishments, whose role it was to train young men to the standard whereby they could receive commissions, produced insufficient numbers. The appalling casualty rate among junior officers was proportionally was far higher than that of their men. With so many new officers urgently required, the pre-war standards of training before commissioning had to be condensed. The young men arriving in France to command platoons were often held in scant regard by their men. Officers promoted from the ranks fared better. Any lack of 'public school' polish was more than compensated for by recent experience in the field of battle.

2/Lt Eric Heaton, 16th Middlesex, killed in action 1 July 1916. Private collection

Definition of Army Formations

British Expeditionary Force (BEF)

This is a global term for all the British Army units in France, Flanders and Italy in the Great War. There were only ever two commanders-in-chief. Until 19 December 1915 Field Marshal Sir John French commanded it. From noon that day General (later Field Marshal) Douglas Haig took over and remained in post for the remainder of the war.

Lines of Communication (Troops)

This term referred to the vast number of soldiers, in hundreds of units in rear areas, dealing with the transport and supply of materials for the fighting soldiers. Their jobs involved working in, at or on: docks, quarries, roads, forestry, railways, repair workshops, general provisions and petrol supply, hospitals, prisons, ambulance trains, hospital ships, etc. The actual lines of communication were the systems of rail, road and navigable waterways linking the army and its base or bases.

Army

An army was an organized body of men armed for war and commanded by a general. It consisted of two or more corps and other supporting units and services including artillery, engineers, medical personnel, veterinary services and transport. By March 1915 there were two armies in the BEF. By 1918 this total had risen to five.

Corps

This was a formation consisting of two or more divisions and also supporting forces, responsible to the lieutenant-general in charge. An army corps's identifying numbers were in Roman numerals.

It is also the name used by units such as Army Service Corps, Royal Army Medical Corps, etc. These two uses of the word 'Corps' must not be confused.

Division

This was almost a miniature army under the command of a major-general. Besides three brigades of combat soldiers, it contained all necessary support units to enable it to fight independently. Such units would include, for example, artillery, ambulance, engineers including a signalling section, and transport. Divisions were frequently moved during the war and came under the command of different corps or armies. There were also cavalry divisions. The regular army in 1914 was comprised of eight divisions, numbered one to eight, but subsequently four more were formed from reservists and men returning from overseas stations. They became the 9th, and 27th to 29th Divisions. Full details of the composition of each division are in the *Order of Battle of Divisions*.

When out of the line a division was usually at rest and/or training. It was re-sorted, reinforced and re-equipped prior to being reassigned to another, perhaps quieter or perhaps not, sector of the front. Brigades were sometimes switched between divisions to bolster a weaker one or to assimilate less experienced troops into a more seasoned one.

Medium and heavy mortar batteries came under divisional control and were operated by men of the Royal Field Artillery. These batteries were usually numbered to correspond to the parent division. For medium batteries, there were normally three, that number was prefixed by X, Y or Z. For the heavy battery the prefix was V.

Brigade (Infantry)

In 1914 it was a formation of four battalions commanded by a brigadier-general and assisted by headquarters staff. A further territorial battalion would sometimes be attached to a brigade. Machine gun and light trench mortar units were controlled at brigade level. Around March 1918 the brigades were reduced in strength from four to three battalions because of shortages of manpower. Several battalions were amalgamated at the same time for the same reason.

Note that the 'Rifle Brigade' is the title of an infantry regiment and consisted of many battalions – it is not a separate brigade. See below.

Regiment

Many soldiers feel they owe allegiance to their regiment. But what exactly is a regiment? It is rather hard to define but simplistically it could be said to be an umbrella organization, steeped in tradition, commanded by a colonel and comprised of battalions of soldiers plus the Depot, regimental silver and the goat or other mascot. Unlike Germany, British regiments never fought as a body. Its battalions were dispersed across the divisions. In peacetime the regular battalions were often on overseas stations and its territorial battalions were spread across their recruiting areas in their respective companies. Only the Depot, with perhaps 100 men, the colonel, goat, etc., remained in the main barracks in its garrison town. But that is where the *esprit de corps* was centred. Soldiers spoke with pride of their regiment and then added that they were in a particular battalion.

Battalion

The infantry battalion was the principal fighting unit of the British Army during the Great War. As part of a brigade, which was in turn part of a division, a battalion was ordinarily commanded by a lieutenant-colonel. He was assisted by twenty-nine officers and a further 977 men made up his command. Thus, notionally, a battalion had 1,007 officers and men. The reality was somewhat different, for battalions often went into battle fielding but a few hundred in total. In addition to the men, a battalion had under its command many horses, wagons and carts to carry ammunition and supplies. The diminutive machine gun section was radically altered as the war progressed. (For details see the Machine Gun Corps.) Infantry battalions frequently moved between brigades during the war. Each battalion was divided into four companies.

New Army battalions were assigned to existing regiments and numbered from where the regular, reserve and territorial battalions ceased, but with the addition of the word 'Service' to their number. Territorial battalions often, but not always, started in the numbering sequence at four and there were often at least two of them. As recruits often elected to join the territorials rather than the regular army (new armies) there were more men than places available. To accommodate this situation new battalions were created and given the same number as the original but with the addition of a prefix. Thus one finds the 1/5th (originally just the 5th), 2/5th and even the 3/5th. Altogether including regular, reserve, territorial, new army, etc. there were 1,743 British infantry battalions during the Great War, but many did not serve overseas.

Not all battalions were primarily comprised of fighting soldiers – although all were armed and fought if required. Several battalions were designated for pioneering or labouring tasks whilst others guarded important installations at home and abroad.

For more information see *British Regiments 1914–1918* (details in Bibliography).

Pals Battalions

It was thought men might more readily enlist if they knew they could serve with their chums – maybe from work or neighbourhood. Men like Lord Derby and the then Major-General Sir Henry Rawlinson appealed for like-minded groups to enlist together. Lord Derby, known as 'England's best recruiting "sergeant"', coined the term 'Pals' when he was recruiting in Liverpool on 28 August 1914. He said: 'this should be a battalion of pals, a battalion in which friends from the same office will fight shoulder to shoulder for the honour of Britain and the credit of Liverpool'. Many similar Pals battalions were formed, with arguably the Accrington Pals being the most well known. Unfortunately, if a Pals Battalion suffered heavy casualties in a battle it meant that a small community at home or at work was particularly hard hit. Whole streets could lose their men-folk overnight.

Cadre
The cadre was a basic unit of a few officers, NCOs and men kept out of the battle, usually with the transport, to form a nucleus for expansion or recovery when necessary, such as when the battalion had devastating losses in battle. The term 'decimated' is often incorrectly used to suppose massive losses; indeed some confuse it with the phrase 'wiped out'. It actually means one man in ten being a casualty. Many units suffered far heavier losses than that.

Company
As one quarter of the fighting arm of a battalion, the company notionally comprised six officers and 221 men. A major or a captain ordinarily commanded the company. Each company was usually titled A, B, C or D. Some battalions however used instead the letters W, X, Y and Z.

Platoon
The platoon was one quarter of a company. A lieutenant or second lieutenant usually commanded it. But frequently in battle an NCO would assume command if the officer was killed.

Section
Each platoon was divided into four sections, each commanded by an NCO.

Artillery (see also Chapters 6 and 8)
The artillery was divided into the Royal Horse, Royal Field and Royal Garrison Artillery. Their batteries were usually classified according to its guns or howitzers. For maximum mobility the Royal Horse Artillery was armed mostly with light guns firing shells weighing 13 pounds. The Royal Field Artillery used slightly heavier 18-pounder field guns plus 4.5" howitzers and some medium artillery pieces. The Royal Garrison Artillery was responsible for heavy guns. There were many titles for these batteries such as horse, field, mountain, garrison, siege, heavy, anti-aircraft and railway. There were also mortar batteries.

Artillery Brigade
An artillery brigade was a grouping of three or four batteries of guns or howitzers commanded, at full strength, by a lieutenant-colonel. To distinguish it from an infantry brigade it was numbered in official writings in Roman numerals. There were usually four or six guns in a battery – sometimes less if the guns were above 12" calibre.

Cavalry

In 1914 there were thirty-one cavalry regiments. They comprised three Household, seven Dragoon Guards, three Dragoons, six Lancers and twelve Hussar Regiments. Technically the dragoons were mounted infantry. In addition there was the Yeomanry, the mounted arm of the Territorial Force. The yeomanry (in a similar fashion to the territorial force) raised second and third line units to reinforce their main regiment. Most of these were later broken up or converted to cyclist or reserve units in 1917, with the men released being retrained accordingly. There was also the Imperial Camel Corps established in 1916, mainly from former Gallipoli veterans.

One cavalry division of four brigades, each comprising three regiments, sailed with the Expeditionary Force in August 1914 but the number of brigades per division was soon reduced to three. Reinforcements for France and Belgium rapidly followed and eventually five cavalry divisions, which incorporated the two Indian divisions, were formed. Three of these remained in service throughout the war. There were additionally dismounted cavalry units.

The regiment was the principal fighting unit of the cavalry. It was commanded by a lieutenant-colonel and comprised around 550 officers and men organized into three squadrons, each of four troops. (The Household Cavalry had four squadrons.) Each regiment also had a two-gun machine gun section and all the men were trained to fight dismounted if necessary. The men were usually armed with the 1908 Pattern Sword plus either a pistol or rifle. A few lancers, as their name implies, still carried eight-foot long lances. Indeed they were used in action at High Wood on the Somme on 14 July 1916.

Medals

These come in two main categories. Campaign medals, or medals for 'being there' and gallantry medals for special deeds of bravery. There were also medals for long service and good conduct, given to men who had served in the armed forces for eighteen years and whose record of service was exemplary. Pre-war regular soldiers often had medals relevant to earlier campaigns such as the 'Boer War' or perhaps, for general service in India.

The precise conditions for the entitlement to any medal, including those briefly mentioned here, are most complex and the subject of specialized books, so these comments are only intended to give general guidance. Again, as with most things in life, there are exceptions to many rules – often because a mistake has been made!

Campaign Medals and Entitlement

For the Great War, each soldier, sailor, airman and certain civilians who served in a defined theatre of war against Germany or her allies was entitled to one or more campaign medals. Where the recipient had been killed, the medals were sent to the next of kin.

The first medal is the bronze 1914 Star that was awarded to those who served in France or Belgium between 5 August and midnight on 22/23 November 1914. Where the serviceman was actually within range of the enemy guns a small bronze bar, to be attached to the medal ribbon, was also awarded. It follows that all those 'Old Contemptibles' killed in action between the above dates in France and Belgium were entitled to the bar. This medal is popularly, if incorrectly, called the Mons Star. Around 378,000 such stars were issued but many, such as those who never left rear areas, were not entitled to the bar.

For those who served in a different theatre of war to that required for the 1914 Star (with or without a bar) or those who did not go to France or Belgium until after 23 November 1914 the appropriate award was a 1914–15 Star. This is very similar to the 1914 Star but was never awarded with a bar to distinguish those who actually served under fire from those

Memorial scroll to 2/Lt Eric Heaton, 16th Middlesex, killed in action 1 July 1916.
Private collection

who worked away from the enemy lines. Only one Star could be held and the 1914–15 Star ceased to be given to anybody who arrived in their theatre of war after 31 December 1915. Members of the Royal Navy, even if killed in the first few days of the war, could only receive the 1914–15 Star unless they served ashore in France or Belgium before 23 November. An example of such service would be with the Royal Naval Division fighting at Antwerp. The medal was made of bronze and approximately 2,366,000 were issued. Of these some 283,500 were for Royal Navy personnel.

A person receiving a 1914 or 1914–15 Star would also be awarded two further campaign medals. The first is the British War Medal, which is made of silver. The criteria for issue were similar to that of the 1914–15 Star but the time in which qualifying service had to count was extended to at least 11 November 1918. In certain theatres this date was extended to as late as 1920 (for example for mine clearance), but the medal is dated 1914–1918.

Memorial plaque to Eric Heaton. Private collection

Those who were sent abroad on or after 1 January 1916 were only eligible for this and the Victory Medal described below. Unless that is, gallantry, long-service awards or special Territorial Force medals were earned. Around 6½ million British War Medals were issued in silver and a further 110,000 in bronze, most often but not always in conjunction with the Victory Medal. The bronze issue was for Chinese, Indian and some other overseas Labour Corps and similar personnel who were paid by the military authorities.

The last campaign medal generally awarded was the Victory Medal, which was cast in bronze to commemorate the Allied victory. Around 5¾ million Victory Medals were despatched. The dates impressed, 1914–1919, reflect the continued fighting in the Middle East, India and Russia into 1919, and the signing of the Peace Treaty at Versailles on 28 June that year.

All campaign medals are named to the recipient and also show his rank/rating and number (unless to an officer, as First World War officers did not have a number), together with the name of his regiment or arm of service. There was no distinction between officers and other ranks regarding the issue of campaign medals.

The medals were sent automatically to the latest address known to the armed forces. It was not necessary to claim them – unlike medals for the Second World War. When the medals were sent to the next of kin because the recipient had been killed, two further items were included. One was a large bronze plaque bearing the dead person's name and inscribed with the words, *He* [or *She*] *Died For Freedom And Honour*. Some 1,355,000 plaques were issued in respect of those who fell during the period 5 August 1914 to 10 January 1920. These were sometimes called 'A Dead Man's Penny'. The other item was a scroll, identical for both officers and men, individually named with additionally rank and regiment.

Silver War Badge

Sometimes called the silver wound badge, it was issued to servicemen honourably discharged from the forces under King's Regulations after September 1916, because of wounds or sickness. Around the front of each badge is written, *For King and Empire. Services Rendered.* Each badge carries a unique number and it is (with some difficulty) possible to trace the recipient from that number. It was issued as a form of recognition to the men who no longer wore a uniform and were being mistaken for those who had never joined up.

Silver war badge.

Gallantry Medals, etc.

There were many instances of gallantry during the Great War. For the deed to be rewarded with a suitable medal or award the recipient usually had to survive the incident. There were certain exceptions. The Victoria Cross and the Albert Medal (the latter for saving or attempting to save life – not necessarily during war) could be awarded posthumously. Details of the heroism are chronicled in the *London Gazette* and are worthwhile reading. Unfortunately the deeds that resulted in the award of the Military Medal were not published in the *Gazette*. There were, no doubt, many other unrecognized acts of heroism, either because the man was killed or because there were no qualified witnesses. If the recipient earned a second (or more) award then a bar(s), to be attached to the ribbon, was given. A brief description of some of the more famous British medals follows but alas space limits me to but a few examples.

Victoria Cross (VC)

It is the premier award for all ranks for supreme acts of gallantry in the face of the enemy. Made from the metal of guns captured from the Russians in the Crimean War, it is simply inscribed with the words, *For Valour.* On the reverse is the date of the deed and on the suspender the recipient's name and unit are engraved. In total 633 Victoria Crosses, including it is believed 293 posthumous awards, were made for the Great War. Only one recipient received both the Victoria Cross and a bar for actions in the First World War. He was Captain Noel Chavasse and he died of his injuries on the second occasion.

Distinguished Service Order (DSO)

First instituted in 1886, it is a decorated, enamelled cross with a crown and laurels in the centre. By the time of the First World War it was more usual for it to be awarded to officers of major (or equivalent rank) and above for distinguished services, usually under fire. Rather less than 9,000 first awards were given to army officers and there were a further 786 bars, including seventy-one second and seven third bars. Naval and Air awards were, in total, 882 and 61 respectively. Both the latter figures include bars. It was not named when issued.

Military Cross (MC)

Instituted on 28 December 1914 and made of silver, it was for captains and lower rank officers and warrant officers, in (Royal) appreciation of 'distinguished and meritorious service in time of war'. Over 37,000 crosses and 4,123 bars – several second and four third bars – were presented. It was not named when issued.

Distinguished Conduct Medal (DCM)

First instituted in 1854, it is a highly regarded decoration for 'other ranks', 'for distinguished conduct in the field'. It ranks below the Victoria Cross but above the Military Medal in prestige. The medal, made of silver, bore the name, rank and number and unit of the recipient and approximately 25,000 (including 470 bars and ten second bars) were awarded during the Great War.

Distinguished Conduct Medal with 1914 Star and Bar, British War and Victory Medals to Sapper Thomas Jones, Royal Engineers, who died of wounds on 15 March 1915. Private collection

Military Medal (MM)

It was felt there was need to reward lesser acts of bravery, for other ranks, than that envisaged for the Distinguished Conduct Medal. In consequence on 25 March 1916 the Military Medal was instituted. It was primarily prescribed 'for bravery in the field' but could also be awarded to women for their bravery. For nearly two months retrospective awards were considered and a few granted. The medal was in silver and bore the name, rank, number and unit of the recipient on the rim. Over 115,000 Military Medals were awarded for the Great War, together with nearly 6,000 bars, including not only 180 second bars but also one third bar – the latter to Corporal E A Corey, 55 Australian Infantry.

Indian Order of Merit (IOM)

Founded in 1837 by the Honourable East India Company, it is the oldest gallantry award of the British Empire. There were two military classes by the time of the Great War. The second class was equivalent to the Distinguished Conduct Medal.

Mentioned in Despatches (MiD)

A 'reward' given by the naming of the recipient in the commander's despatch to higher authority and then published in the *London Gazette*. Along with the Victoria Cross and Albert Medal, and unlike the other awards, the MiD could be made posthumously. To symbolize the Mention a sprig of bronze oak leaves was worn on the ribbon of the Victory Medal and a special certificate was issued. Nearly 140,000 army personnel were 'Mentioned in Despatches' for the First World War.

Regimental Numbers

At the beginning of the Great War – and indeed before it – many soldiers were issued with an identical service number to that already in use by men from other units. Unique army numbers were not issued until at least 1920 (and then only for the Army Reserve and new soldiers) and only an overview of the Great War numbering system is possible here. Essentially each army corps, e.g. Royal Engineers, Royal Artillery, etc., and each infantry battalion was allocated a block of numbers to issue, ranging from one to several thousand. As regiments usually had more than one regular battalion, duplication occurred even within that regiment. Sometimes a number prefix was used to distinguish the battalion (e.g. 3/3321) but that practice was not universal. It was also confusing where a man changed battalions within a regiment but often kept his old number! If he moved to another regiment he was allocated a new number. It is obvious therefore that much duplication occurred. Indeed, using *Soldiers Died in the Great War* as a reference source, it is noticed that even the number 'one' had been issued to eight different soldiers who died. Although not having the highest instance of overall repetition, when compared with some other numbers, over 220 British soldiers were issued with the number 1883. And of those thirty-seven died during the war – more than with any other number.

Territorial battalions followed a similar system until 1 March 1917 when they were renumbered using six-figure numbers, starting at 200,001 under the provisions of Army Council Instruction 2414 of December 1916. Unfortunately even after this exercise much duplication occurred, as each army administrative record office seems to have issued blocks of numbers that replicated those issued by other record offices. Even the number of 200,001 appears to have been issued to seventy-eight soldiers. The problem of insufficient unique numbers was not properly addressed and we were not much better off than before.

Various prefixes were added to numbers and each had different meanings. Concerning the infantry, not all regiments used all of the prefixes and there were variations and errors by record offices when issuing numbers. There were many other letters used and in consequence the following is only a guide and is certainly not complete.

L	Regular Army – line regiments
G	General
GS	General Service
GSSR	General Service Special Reserve
SR	Special Reserve (former regular soldiers)
S	Similar to GS prefix and mainly, but not exclusively intended for Scottish Regiments
TF	Territorial Force

The Army Service Corps especially used prefixes to indicate the branch of the Corps to which a man was attached. The main branches and number prefixes were:

Remount	R/
Supply	S/
Horse Transport	T/
Mechanical Transport	M/

A second letter prefix was frequently added to indicate the trade or other subcategory to which the man belonged.

Other prefixes were used by battalions of certain regiments to indicate the original recruiting source. For example:

SD   Southdown Battalions (11, 12 and 13/Royal Sussex Regiment).
PS   Public Schools Battalion (16/Middlesex Regiment.
STK Stockbrokers Battalion (10/Royal Fusiliers)

Sadly, because of the duplication referred to earlier, it is rarely possible to positively identify a First World War soldier from his basic number alone if that is all you have.

Chapter 3

THE NEW SOLDIER

Why Enlist?

Life in Britain for most people, just before the Great War, was not easy. Many children died young and the male life expectancy was only 50. Health and safety laws scarcely existed and thousands died each year in industrial and agricultural accidents. Trade unions had little muscle and it was rare for any compensation to be paid to widows or mutilated survivors. With no wireless (radio) in the home, newspapers reigned supreme over the distribution of information, which was not entirely unbiased. Wages were poor, malnutrition commonplace and any entertainment mostly home-grown.

Is it any wonder men were eager to escape their dull and drab existence for the adventure the army was offering? They were assured a dependable, if not generous, wage; they were regularly fed with often far better food than at home; they were clothed and housed. And, perhaps for the first time in their lives, adventure beckoned. They could travel to foreign parts and become part of the infectious patriotic surge that was sweeping the land.

These men were not natural heroes but they were certainly not cowards either. Their country needed them – all the newspapers, billboards and propaganda told them so. Their conditions at home were not exactly wonderful. And so they flocked to the Colours in their hundreds of thousands. The famous pointing finger of Lord Kitchener advising people that 'Your country needs you' drew in recruits for the army; other posters set about attracting men to the navy. One thing Britain has always been good at is propaganda and in wartime it excels itself.

Attestation

Attestation is essentially an oath of allegiance to the monarch and country. Pre-war, to join the regular army, the would-be soldier had to comply with certain formalities including fairly strict physical requirements. He had to be aged between 19 and 38, at least 5 foot 3 inches tall, and physically fit. He could generally choose his regiment and committed himself for twelve years service with the Colours and on Reserve. There were other avenues into the army such as the Territorial Force or Special Reserve.

When war broke out, the flood of volunteers initially overwhelmed the system and shortcuts were taken. The man had to pass a rudimentary interview by the recruiting sergeant and then, after a basic medical examination, fill in an attestation form in duplicate. It was commonly, but not exclusively, Army Form B.111 that committed the soldier to serve 'until the War is over'. He then swore an oath of allegiance to the King before an officer. The wartime medical was not usually too demanding and the Army Form B.178, completed by the medical officer, included a physical description of the soldier. Another officer then certified his approval and at that stage the man was deemed to be a soldier subject to the King's Regulations. He then received a shilling. Usually the recruit was sent home to await call-up for training.

THE WATCHERS OF THE SEAS.

THE NAVY NEEDS BOYS AND MEN FROM 15 TO 40 YEARS OF AGE.

APPLY: 7, WHITEHALL PLACE, S.W.

Royal Navy recruiting poster dated 1915 (by L. Raven-Hill).

Soldiers were classified into medical groups depending upon their health and age. The basic categories were A, B, C or D with subcategories added in numbers, e.g. A1, B2, C1, etc. Essentially all A group were medically fit for active service overseas. Those in group B were fit for lines of communication duties overseas; those in group C were assigned to home service duties, whilst those in group D were, at least in the short term, considered unfit for any normal military duties but could work in depots at home. The precise criteria, including height restrictions, became somewhat blurred during the course of the war to suit manpower requirements. Indeed Bantams battalions were soon created to cater for shorter but fit men over 5 feet tall.

Over/Under Age and Aliases

There are so many accounts of men attesting under age that either there is mass hysteria on the subject or some truth in it! The army did not officially encourage under-age enlistment but, on the other hand, did not insist on proof of age at the recruiting centre. On the Military History Sheet age is referred to as 'Apparent Age' and on Army Form B.178 (Medical History) it is described as 'declared age'. The subject does not appear to have been of vital importance to the military. Interestingly, of the seventeen questions on army attestation Form B.111, only eleven were subject to a penalty (two years hard-labour) if a false

The grave of Henry Webber, one of but by no means the oldest soldier to die for his country.

statement was made. The first six questions, which included name, nationality and age, were exempt from that penalty if untruthfully answered. And those are the main areas where lies were told. Indeed, over 6,000 British Empire men died under an assumed name and the number enlisting under or over age is totally unknown but not inconsequential.

Aside from a few '(very) old soldiers' serving in the United Kingdom, probably in an administrative capacity, the proven extremes for those who died on active service are 15 and 69. (The true age of a famous 14-year-old casualty is not proven.) But then we have Field Marshal Lord Roberts VC who died whilst inspecting his troops in France at the age of 82.

Pay and Allotment

The basic rate of pay for a private soldier was one shilling per day. This could be increased by earning proficiency pay in various skills, such as marksmanship. An increase of one (old) penny was paid when in a war zone. From 29 September 1917 a further three (old) pence per day was given by way of a pay increase. If the soldier was in one of the corps, such as Royal Engineers or Army Service Corps, then he would have been paid more for his specialist skills such as mining or mechanical vehicle driving. If the soldier was married it was usual for an allotment or compulsory

Notification under A.O. 1, of 4-12-17 of alteration of the net rate of pay issuable to a soldier from the 29th September, 1917.

(To be inserted in front of page 3 of A.B. 64.)

Soldier's Name. *[handwritten]*

Regtl. No. and Rank. *Pte 51217*

Unit. **ROYAL FUSILIERS**

	s.	d.
Regimental Pay (including the extra 3d. a day authorised for Warrant and N.C.Os. of certain arms)	1	—
Proficiency Pay		3
Service Pay		
Engineer or Corps Pay		
Difference (if any) to make up the minimum under the Army Order		3
War Pay		1
Deduct Voluntary Allotment		
Compulsory Stoppage		
† NET DAILY RATE FOR ISSUE :		

(Words). *[handwritten] One Shilling Sevenpence* 1 7

[stamp] JAN 19.. ....Date.

[signature] Regimental Paymaster.

....................................Station.

† Subject to Promotions, Reductions, etc., since 29th Sept., 1917.

[M4001] W2683/G331 500m 12/17

Page of soldier's pay book (Army book 64).

stoppage of six (old) pence per day to be paid to his wife. This was supplemented and the wife of a private or corporal received 12/6d per week, with more for children. If he was not married he could nominate one dependent relative to receive (a lesser sum of) money. Many conditions were imposed. More was paid for sergeants and warrant officers but they had to contribute more as well.

Currency Guide (Approximate)

1 shilling = 12 (old) pence or 5 (new) pence (one shilling was shown as 1/-)
1 (old) penny = ½ (new) pence (one old penny was shown as 1d)
Thus 1/6½d was one shilling and six pence ha'penny (8 (new) pence) and 12/6d was twelve shillings and six pence (62½ (new) pence).

We must however realize that one shilling in 1914 was worth approximately £3.44 in today's values – a sixty-nine-fold increase due to inflation. The average weekly unskilled wage was then £1/5/0d, equal to £86.25 in 2008. However his rent took less than a quarter of his wage and he could buy a kilo (2.2lbs) of flour for around three old pence and beef was cheap at nine old pence a kilo. Good beer was six old pence a pint and cigarettes three old pence for a packet of twenty!

Training

Basic training for the new recruit was divided into two unequal parts. The soldier had to become fit, learn about his equipment, and be taught how to shoot and fight with a bayonet, as well as learn the basic skills to prepare him for war. Initially, however, the most intensive part of his training was designed to instil unquestioned discipline and build up his physique. For this, seemingly endless marching, drill and polishing of equipment were imposed. The precise method of saluting was judged to be of prime importance. The soldier had to obey orders unchallenged and immediately as if it were second nature. Accurate drill requires immediate response to a word of command and, if repeated often enough, men became accustomed to the routine of blind obedience. Individual initiative was most certainly discouraged at this level of training. Minor transgressions resulted in extra drill or fatigues. More serious breaches of discipline resulted in detention in one form or other.

Formal marching, with arms raised shoulder height on every step, is considered by the army to be excellent overall exercise. To toughen them up, men went on route marches of from fifteen to twenty-five miles a day, carrying their full pack and rifle or, in the parlance of the day, 'full marching order'. The usual pace or step for marching was thirty inches and troops marched at the rate of three miles per hour with short halts being permitted. Rivers were considered fordable up to a depth of three feet. No allowance at all was made for wet clothing and boots afterwards!

The second part of the training was spent learning the basics of army life. Particular attention was paid to the correct use of the bayonet and elementary shooting skills were practised on the rifle ranges. Fire discipline – when and what and how to shoot was taught. The pre-war standards of marksmanship (fifteen accurately aimed shots per minute) had to be abandoned for new recruits, as time was critical. After 1914 some instruction was given on trench digging and on life in the trenches.

More advanced training was often carried out in the theatre of war – especially so if it were France and Flanders. Soldiers usually spent many unhappy hours in training camps such as the famous Bull Ring at Etaples. It was in such places that they learnt some of the finer arts of trench warfare and were subject to even more rigorous drill routines to hone their discipline. Courses were given to newly arrived men on the art of killing without being killed, by soldiers with recent practical experience. Specialist courses were also run from bases such as Rouen, Harfleur, Havre and Etaples for newly appointed NCOs and officers on matters as diverse as bombing, machine-gunning, mapping, signalling, etc. Before major offensives, rehearsals were sometimes practised in specially constructed training battlefield areas.

The minutiae of killing were taught, as the following extract from a 1918 War Office training pamphlet on the use of the bayonet illustrates:

> If possible the point of the bayonet should be directed against the opponent's throat, especially in corps-d-corps fighting, as the point will enter easily and make a fatal wound on penetrating a few inches and, being near the eyes, makes an opponent 'funk'. Other vulnerable and usually exposed parts are the face, chest, lower abdomen and thighs, and the region of the kidneys when the back is turned. Four to six inches' penetration is sufficient to incapacitate and allow for a quick withdrawal, whereas if the bayonet is driven home too far it is often impossible to withdraw it. In such cases a round should be fired to break up the obstruction.

Embarkation

Infantry battalions were gradually formed into divisions and they assembled ready for deployment to a theatre of war by troopship, usually from one of the Channel ports. There are published lists showing their initial date of arrival. If the soldier went to war before 31 December 1915 the area he was sent to and the date of arrival should be shown on his Medal Index Card.

Wills

A soldier on active service was able to make a simple will in his pay book. It did not need to be witnessed and was usually honoured.

12

Short Form of Will.

(See instruction 4 on page 1).

If a soldier on active service, or under orders for active service, wishes to make a short will, he may do so on the opposite page. **It must be entirely in his own handwriting and must be signed by him and dated.** The full names and addresses of the persons whom he desires to benefit, and the sum of money or the articles or property which he desires to leave to them, must be clearly stated. **The mere entry of the name of an intended legatee on the opposite page without any mention of what the legatee is to receive is of no legal value.**

The following is a specimen of a will leaving all to one person :—

In the event of my death I give the whole of my property and effects to my mother, Mrs. Mary Atkins, 999, High Street, Aldershot.
(Signature) THOMAS ATKINS.
Private, No. 1793,
Date, 5th August, 1914.   Gloucester Fusrs.

The following is a specimen of a will leaving legacies to more than one person :—

In the event of my death I give £10 to my friend, Miss Rose Smith, of No. 1, High Street, London, and I give £5 to my sister, Miss Sarah Atkins, 999, High Street, Aldershot, and I give the remaining part of my property to my mother, Mrs. Mary Atkins, 999, High Street, Aldershot.
(Signature) THOMAS ATKINS,
Private, No. 1793,
Date, 5th August, 1914.   Gloucester Fusrs.

13

WILL.

In the event of myself meeting my death dureing the period of war I leave all belongings and money due to me. to my wife. Violet King. 37 Glouster. Rd. Brighton. Sussex.

Signature _Edward King._

Rank & Regiment _P E R. Fs. 51217_

Date _30/10/16._

Will made on active service (part of pay book). The instruction on p. 1 reads 'When you have been placed under orders for active service (and not before) you may make your will, if so desired.'

Uniforms and Accoutrements

Because of the huge influx of men in 1914 it was not possible to clothe and arm them to current specifications straight away. Around 500,000 recruits wore improvised uniforms during training, made from blue serge, and popularly known as 'Kitchener's Blues'. Blue was substituted as the traditional khaki dye came from Germany, whose chemical industry specialized in dyes. It was naturally unobtainable once war commenced and it took a while to find a replacement. Many varieties of 'uniform' and other kit existed, especially early in the war when much was purchased hurriedly from America and Canada. Even the manufacture of the tunic was simplified for mass production but all had a field dressing enclosed in a special inside pocket. Headgear also changed from the formal cap to much more comfortable hats. The 'Gor Blimy' soft cap, with flaps to keep the ears warm, was very popular, but was gradually replaced by a new soft cap in 1916.

Old rifles and other items were unearthed from reserve stores and issued to fill the gap until more could be made. The term 'accoutrements' is defined as comprising those items, other than weapons, carried outside the clothing. It consisted of belts, pouches, bandoliers, slings, mess tins, haversacks, water bottles and similar articles. Some of this is technically called 'equipment', i.e. the harness and containers used to carry all the items a soldier needed. It had been made of webbing since 1908 but was complex to produce rapidly, so leather items were substituted.

The full kit list for a soldier was most impressive and covered items from his studded boots to his cap. When marching during training he carried over 61 pounds (28kg) of clothing, weapons and equipment. Everything seemed heavy. The rifle, bayonet and 150 rounds of ammunition weighed almost 20lbs (9kg). Even his woollen underpants (drawers) weighed over one pound (500g). And that was when they were clean and fresh on! Occasionally as much as a month would elapse between changes. Here kilted regiments gained – they were not issued with any. Additional items, such as a steel helmet and respirator, were added as time went by.

Marching: Time and Distance

For the infantry soldier the usual mode of transport was his feet. Only rarely did he get a ride. Indeed, during the course of the war the British army wore out over 40 million pairs of boots!

The usual infantry marching speed was at the rate of 98 yards per minute or three miles per hour. That allowed for a six-minute halt every hour. Infantry soldiers marched in columns of four abreast and each battalion (notionally 1,007 officers and men) took up 590 yards of road space for the fighting portion, with a further 210 yards allocated to their first line transport. A battalion therefore occupied 800 yards of road – not far short of half a mile – while on the move. In 1914 a division, which was home to around 18,000 officers and men, plus 5,000 horses and hundreds of wagons and carts took up nearly fifteen miles of road space if it ever moved as a complete unit. Small columns of seasoned troops could cover twenty-five miles a day in favourable conditions. Larger groups, hampered by transport wagons, were expected to travel fifteen miles per day.

Column of soldiers moving by the usual means of transport – marching. Paul Reed Archives

Identity Discs

The British Army issued official identity discs from at least 1906. Initially the single disc was made of aluminium and then, from 1914, a red compressed fibre disc gradually superseded it. By September 1916 it was decided two discs were required. A round disc, whether the earlier aluminium or later red fibre type, was to remain on the body after burial. The second fibre disc, which had eight sides and was dull green in colour, was to be removed in the event of death and the details recorded. The information stamped into the discs was basically surname, initials, number, unit and religion but variations appeared. Each belligerent nation had a different design of identity disc. The fibre discs endured for a long time in the ground. But no one expected them to last for around a century, which is one reason why recently discovered bodies can rarely be identified. The term 'dog-tag' was not used in the Great War. Soldiers referred to the identity disc as a 'cold meat ticket'. Many soldiers had private identity discs or bracelets made from all manner of materials, but coins seem to have been the most popular.

Examples of official identity discs.

Home Leave

This was at the discretion of the officer commanding the unit and depended for other ranks on the manpower available and to a large extent on the soldier's service record. Denial of home leave was used as a punishment for transgressions. There do not seem to have been any fixed criteria until mid-1917 but it was not unusual for a couple of years to elapse before leave was granted. Transport by train and boat was free but there was a problem. Any leave pass was for a fixed number of days, often as few as five, and the amount allotted included the time it took to travel to and from home. That was fine for a soldier who lived in Dover but not so good for the man whose address was in Scotland. And getting from the trenches to the railway station could be time-consuming. Officers seem to have received a more generous allowance.

All kit, including his rifle but not usually ammunition, was taken home by the soldier. This was because his unit may well have moved by the time of his return and there were no facilities to store and transport extra kit. Any spare space in his pack was usually crammed with souvenirs, such as cap badges, *pickelhaubes*, fuse caps, etc., picked up on the battlefields. It was not unusual for more deadly items to be brought back. Among the souvenirs was often a lice-infested uniform for his mother to launder.

Chapter 4

THE TRENCH

Trenches: Summary

A trench was effectively a slot dug into the ground. Its purpose was to limit the effect of different projectiles and the blast effect of high explosive shells. They were the most common type of defensive position on the battlefields. The first real trenches, which were to form the opposing lines for well over three years of siege warfare on the Western Front, were constructed in September 1914 following the Allied Advance to the Aisne. Before that, during the period of mobile warfare, when necessary individual soldiers dug hollows in the ground with their entrenching tools to get some protection from incoming small arms and artillery fire. (An entrenching tool is a personal issue small spade that frequently incorporated a short pick.) The ideal textbook front-line trench was about 3 feet 4 inches wide at the top, around 7 feet deep with the sides cut as steep as possible, and tapering to about 3 feet wide at the bottom. It had raised areas at the front and back, known respectively as a parapet and a parados. About 18 inches of the width at the bottom incorporated a raised fire-step on the side facing the enemy. It did not leave much actual floor space for movement. The exact construction varied considerably and was heavily dependent upon the soil conditions. Often the sides were reinforced with corrugated iron, wickerwork hurdles, wire netting, timber or other convenient materials scavenged locally. Where sandbags were used, they were laid to precise specifications and stakes were driven through them at intervals to add strength and avoid collapse. Sandbags were normally only used where speed of construction was the first priority as they rotted after a while and in consequence their contents spilled out into the trench. In general terms

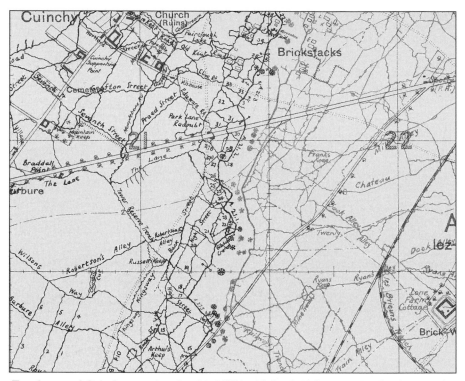

Trench map of Cuinchy area (number 36c NW1 and dated 10 June 1916), showing opposing lines. Note craters in NML.

the narrower the trench, the more protection it offered. After the lessons learnt at the beginning of the war, the trench bottoms were often floored with duckboards to aid travel and drainage of water.

Some trenches were at least partially covered with material to afford some protection from descending shrapnel and shell fragments, as well as the worst of the weather. The cover also made the trench more difficult to spot from the air. They were not popular however and most trenches – including all front-line trenches – were totally exposed to the elements. This of course risked death or harm from exposure. Outside the trench, earth was built up at both the front and rear. Often carefully but unevenly laid sandbags were used for this purpose. Dummy trenches were also dug to confuse and entrap any invading enemy.

In Belgium and the northern parts of France the water table is very high – often only one or two feet below the surface. In these conditions it was not

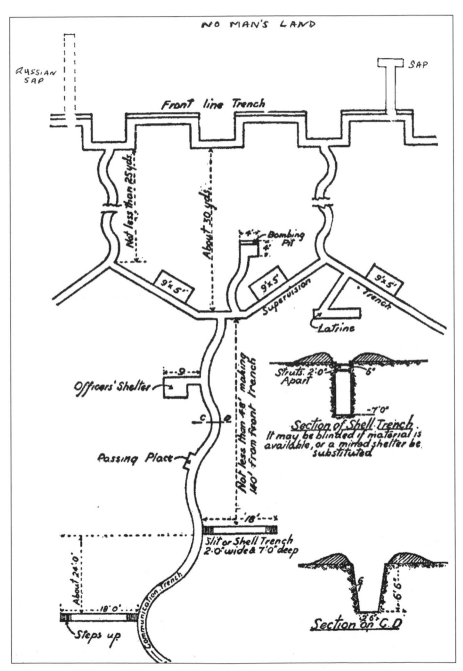

Sketch showing typical trench system.

practical to dig deep trenches. Instead a shallow trench was dug and then earth built up in front of the trench to form high breastworks and thus give as much protection as possible. Most trenches were a compromise between the two main types.

Trenches were initially dug by infantry soldiers, mostly under cover of darkness. Later in the war planned trench lines – as opposed to the majority that evolved due to prevailing circumstances – were often dug by labour battalions or even members of the Labour Corps. Whenever possible the trenches were profiled to afford maximum concealment. From the diagram it will be seen that the trench system was comprised of several elements, some of which are briefly described below. Despite seeming haphazard, trenches were very carefully thought out to give the best possible protection to their occupants, whilst affording a good field of fire with which to engage the enemy. Their mutual support capacity with nearby emplacements was vital and consideration was also paid to their drainage potential. It was not desirable that soldiers should stand in waterlogged trenches if it could be avoided. Some trenches were on the reverse slope of a prominence to improve their defensive capabilities. These required forward saps for observation and to act as fire-bays. Dead ground, that is, an area which cannot be covered by fire, was avoided at all costs. It could provide cover for an attacking force. Small excavations were frequently dug into the rear wall of the trench to contain a small fireplace for heating water and cooking breakfast. The schematic diagram of a trench system includes many of these terms.

Defence in Depth

As the war progressed, more and more lines of trenches were dug as the technique of 'defence in depth' evolved. The Germans were the first to use this system. Some trenches were many hundreds of yards behind the front, which was only lightly defended. An invader would be gradually drawn into progressively more heavily defended zones. Each layer would give way in turn, inflicting casualties before its garrison retreated. The attacking forces would additionally be subjected to enfilading fire from the flanks and would be continually expending its limited ammunition supplies. Meanwhile the defender fell back behind new fortified lines upon fresh and unlimited supplies. As the layers of trenches could stretch back miles in some cases, the attacker may well have been unaware of their existence and run out of fighting capacity before breaching the final line. With the old system, once the front and support trenches were broken through, there was little to stop the invader.

Elements of a Trench or Trench System

Barbed Wire
Inescapably linked to the maze of trench systems, and defending them from easy infiltration, were huge swathes of barbed wire. By 1915 these were not simple strands such as found surrounding fields at home but vast entanglements designed to be impenetrable. Belts of barbed wire stretched along much of the Western Front on both sides of No Man's Land and it was regarded as both a blessing to be behind and a barrier to try to penetrate – depending upon whose wire one was contemplating.

The wire was fixed in position by vast quantities of stakes driven into the ground or suspended from specially designed screw-pickets. Coils of wire were expanded and fixed to the stakes. Another method, when rapid wiring was required, was the use of chevaux-de-frise – a preconstructed obstacle of posts and barbed wire that could be carried into position, dumped and staked there.

The belts of wire varied enormously in height and depth but ideally were about 3 feet high and over 30 feet in depth (10m). Usually, a second band of similar dimensions was laid parallel to and further out from the first to keep enemy bombers at bay. Very often there was yet a third entanglement with a gap between it and the preceding one. A distance of around twenty yards from the front-line was generally left free of wire. These bands of intermeshed wire were so dense that they clearly show on aerial photographs taken from several thousand feet altitude. Single strands of wire, with tin cans containing stones suspended from them, were often set a few inches from the ground some distance from the front-line trench. It was designed to catch an intruder attempting infiltration by night and attract the attention of sentries.

At night parties would frequently go out to try to penetrate the enemy's wire and gather intelligence. Samples of the enemy wire were taken for analysis. Again, each night men would be sent out to repair and strengthen their own wire. Sometimes this led to confusion. In one instance, the then Lieutenant Philip Neame (15 Field Company Royal Engineers) sent a verbal message to supporting infantry, 'The R.E. are going out to wire. Don't fire.'

The message that finally reached the machine guns was: 'Enemy in the wire. Open fire.' The resulting mêlée, with both sides soon shooting at the unfortunate sappers, can well be imagined.

Before a major assault, gaps were made in one's own entanglements to allow the troops through. The gaps were zigzagged in such a way as to be invisible from the enemy positions and marked out with tapes. Various methods were tried to destroy enemy wire defences but none were entirely successful. At best the wire was partially cut but still represented a considerable obstacle for the soldiers trying to get through it. High explosive shells usually lifted the wire into the air and dumped it back on the ground in a jumbled heap, making it more difficult to cut and cross through than the original. Developments in fuse design made the shattering of areas of barbed wire possible with certain mortar bombs, but that depended upon great accuracy and the opposing wire being relatively close. Another method used was to fire shrapnel shells set to burst just over the wire to attempt to cut it with the shrapnel balls ejected. None of these techniques worked well in action and they consumed vast quantities of shells and bombs in the process. Time after time advancing soldiers reported the supposedly well-cut wire to still be a major obstacle that had to be cut manually with wire cutters of varying descriptions. The eventual use of tanks to drag the wire away was probably the best method discovered in the war.

Trench constructed almost entirely with sand bags.

Berm
This was a small flat space left between the rising parapet and the drop of the forward trench wall. It helped stop the parapet collapsing into the trench and also served as a place to keep spare ammunition, etc.

Bombing Pit/Trench
A short sap, often from the command trench, ending in a small pit a few feet square. It was located within grenade-throwing distance of the front-line in order that our bombers could attack any enemy who had occupied our front-line. It was well stocked with grenades for that purpose in a reinforced bomb store.

Bomb Store
Besides those in bombing pits, supplies of grenades (bombs) were kept nearby in communication trenches for the use of raiding parties and specially trained bombers. More were stored at the front to repel boarders.

Breastworks
Similar to parapets but built up higher above ground to protect soldiers standing in a shallow trench that could not be dug deeper.

Communication Trenches
These were dug to link the various trench systems running parallel with the front-line. They enabled troops from rear areas to reinforce the front-line garrison without exposing themselves to enemy fire. To defend against enfilade fire and the effect of shells bursting in them they were usually zigzagged or undulating throughout their length. They were often congested and at times soldiers climbed out and proceeded on the surface. Whilst this practice was reasonably safe at night it was very dangerous during daylight hours. Communication trenches were also used to bring up rations and replacement battalions.

Duckboards
Joined slats of wood laid on the floor of trenches to keep the soldiers' feet out of the worst of the mud and water. Beneath them there was usually a channel cut to carry away water to a sump from where it could (sometimes) be pumped away.

Dugouts

There were several types of 'dugout' depending upon its purpose. As a general principle, the British did not construct substantial subterranean bunkers, as they considered that any shelters were purely for very temporary accommodation. After defeating the enemy they would no longer be required. That is the exact opposite philosophy to the Germans who planned to stay in situ and consequently built very strong and comparatively comfortable fortifications. Theirs were often equipped with electric light and furniture taken from nearby houses.

Officers' shelters were constructed underground so that they would have a place for administrative work and a centre for local communications. It was essential that protection be afforded from the weather and light artillery fire.

Most dugouts were of a similar construction. Often curved corrugated iron sheets, known as elephant iron, were used to form the basis of the shelter. The roof was next usually reinforced with logs, railway lines or other such material that might be found locally. It was then covered with earth and then rubble to burst incoming shells, followed by as much compacted earth as possible to give greater security and to disguise its existence from aerial observation. Great care was taken that buried telephone lines and approach routes radiating towards it did not betray its presence. The doorways (usually at least two) would be protected from gas ingress by heavy and wet curtains made from blankets, etc. These also served to stop any glimmer of light escaping.

Shelters were also constructed as aid posts and to disguise emplacements for weapons such as machine guns, mortars and artillery pieces. These varied enormously in design and many were simply pure camouflage whereas others were fairly deep. Few British shelters offered more than scant protection from a direct hit from anything heavier than medium shells.

Soldiers generally got by in the fire-trenches with little or no shelter. The front faces of trenches were sometimes excavated, to make a small recess that a man might squeeze into when not on duty. Care had to be taken that the hollowing out did not weaken the trench and cause a collapse that might bury the recumbent soldier. In general the practice was discouraged. Support and reserve lines back from the front and artillery positions, etc., were often equipped with deeper shelters for men off-duty to afford protection from shelling. Whatever form of dugout was constructed it was common practice to hang any uneaten food from the roof in sandbags to deter rats. Rodents were a constant menace for besides stealing food they feasted upon rotting corpses, both animal and human. Their droppings were everywhere and they were a major cause of the spread of diseases. Because of the plentiful supply of food they bred at prodigious rates and the size they grew to is the stuff of legends.

Enfilade

Trenches were designed to avoid, if at all possible, enfilade fire. The word comes the French 'enfiler', meaning to skewer. It is slightly complex but generally means fire directed along the longest axis of the target. It could be shots fired along the length of a trench from one end to the other; or along the length of a body of advancing soldiers; or raking fire against the flank of a column of men crossing in front. Because it offers such an opportunity to inflict maximum damage it is to be strictly avoided. Trenches were zigzagged to prevent more than a short length being vulnerable to enfilade fire.

Fire-Step

An earth shelf forming part of the wall of the trench, on the side facing the enemy, for the sentry to stand on at night and see out across No Man's Land. During daylight hours men sat or lay upon it to rest and thus not obstruct the narrow trench floor. If an enemy trench was taken over it had to be modified with a new fire-step cut into the opposite wall. For this purpose several soldiers carried rather large and heavy army spades and picks when attacking the enemy in battle. Even more were similarly equipped to create extra trenches in captured ground.

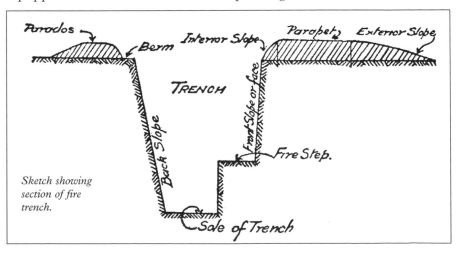

Sketch showing section of fire trench.

Front-Line

This was in two elements. The very front-line, which was called the fire-trench, could be continuous or made up of 'linked' shell holes or saps forming fire-bays. Where it was continuous, although never straight, the line was revetted for strength and often castellated to form traverses. A reserve of ammunition was readily available. Machine guns were usually strategically hidden there to be able to sweep the whole of No Man's Land. No shelters or overhead cover were permitted in the front-line.

The second element was the command or supervision trench. It was around thirty yards behind the fire-trench, and regularly linked to it. From there immediate help was available in the shape of additional concealed machine guns and bomb throwers sited in pits.

Keep

A strongpoint offering all-round defence and shelter to its garrison. Some parts of the front relied upon this method of accommodating troops rather than locating large bodies of men in the front-line. When necessary, the men streamed out along a web of communication trenches towards the front or other areas in need of reinforcement.

Latrines

One of the quickest ways to get infectious diseases was by contamination from untreated excreta. The British Army was very keen on trench hygiene. Latrines or field toilets were constructed to carefully considered designs at the end of short saps near to many of the lines. They were pits, often dug over five or six feet deep, and the faeces deposited were rapidly covered with a little earth, cresol solution or quicklime. Sometimes buckets, emptied each night, were used instead. A more biologically efficient type of latrine required that a short trench be dug to no more than one foot deep and filled as soon as possible. It may have been efficient but was more exposed and not greatly appreciated by men requiring a toilet close to enemy fire.

Each infantry company appointed two of its number to act as sanitary personnel who were excused normal duties in exchange for keeping the latrines in good condition and emptying urine buckets properly. The job of 'shit-wallah', as the sanitary men were affectionately known, was actually a sought-after appointment as it kept them away from the dangers of the front-lines for much of the time.

As for toilet paper – there was none. Some officers may have had a private supply but there was no official issue. Letters from home were never wasted but recycled! That is the reason why, whilst literally thousands of letters *from* soldiers to home survive in archives, there are almost none sent *to* soldiers abroad and subsequently brought back. As a veteran once said to me, 'we were country boys – maybe a tuft of grass; maybe nothing'. I doubt much grass was available in the trenches!

Loopholes

The parapets of traverses were periodically pierced obliquely at irregular intervals with loopholes gouged or built into them. These holes were disguised and camouflaged to avoid detection by the enemy. Their purpose was for observation, sighting of machine guns and sniping during the day. The observer was often partially protected from enemy sniper fire by bullet-proof (one centimetre thick) steel plates covering the gap. These plates, in turn, had a loophole in them that could be covered by a metal flap. It was vital also that the observer was shielded from behind so that no light came past him to be seen through the loophole. This would easily be seen from the enemy trenches and give away his location.

No Man's Land

The area between the opposing forces. It evolved rather than was planned and the distances between the two front-lines ranged from a few yards to half a mile or more in places. Sometimes it was so narrow that bombs could be thrown into opposing trenches and conversations easily overheard. It was frequently explored at night by each side's patrols seeking intelligence or enemy prisoners. The attitude of at least one senior officer, who maintained that there was no such thing as No Man's Land and that the front-line was the German wire, did not help. Whilst perhaps it was understandable, to keep up pressure on the enemy, it no doubt contributed considerably to the growing nightly casualty list in an attempt to fulfil that approach.

Parados

The build-up of earth above the rear of the trench was called the parados. Its purpose was twofold. It protected the trench from the blast of shells exploding at its rear. Additionally, it prevented soldiers on sentry duty standing on the fire-step from forming silhouettes against the skyline and thus presenting easy targets. In general terms the front-lines ran north–south. Each morning the sun rose behind the German lines and each evening it set behind the British lines. Each side therefore would have been exposed on the skyline in turn if a parados was not constructed.

Parapet

Earth was built up above the ground in front of the trench facing the enemy. It was called the parapet. It would be about one foot high and several feet broad before sloping towards the ground at around a 45-degree angle. The slope was designed to help deflect bullets and the blast of shells upward. The purpose of the parapet was to shield the sentry standing on his fire-step and generally add strength to the trench. For it to stop a bullet from a rifle or machine gun the parapet needed to be five feet thick if made from clay. Other soil types offered greater protection, especially if they were very stony or made from compacted sand. The height of the parapet depended largely upon the depth of the trench, which could vary considerably.

Periscopes

These were a vital trench tool used to see over the parapet during daylight hours and survive. Some were professionally manufactured whilst others were improvised by using pieces of salvaged mirror fixed in a wooded frame. Snipers shot at periscopes, as well as imprudent heads. Dummy periscopes were made so that the path of the bullet could be traced and perhaps the position of the sniper revealed.

Pill Boxes and Bunkers

These were strong steel-reinforced concrete constructions to supplement trench systems, especially where continuous lines were not possible. Their existence enabled fewer men to be employed guarding a section of front for they usually had great firepower from machine guns and were difficult and dangerous to neutralize.

Reserve Line

This was perhaps 500 yards behind the front and consisted of conventional trenches, linked redoubts or dugouts, holding reserve soldiers available to form a counter-attack if the front was over-run.

Reserve Trench System

These were successive lines of trenches similar in design to the front-line and linked to it and each other by communication trenches. There were often several lines of trenches some distance behind the front. They were not however so far apart that each line could not support its neighbour.

Sap

Usually a short cul-de-sac trench dug out from a main position – generally, but not always, from the front-line and into No Man's Land – for the purposes of observation and as a listening post. They were originally devised as a method of approaching a fortified position within the relative safety of a trench that was progressed towards the enemy. The man who dug saps was known as a 'sapper'.

A 'Russian sap' was similar to a sap but dug below ground level in the form of a shallow tunnel. When close enough for its purpose it would break through to the surface.

Shell Trench or Slit Trench

Short, narrow and deep trenches coming off communication trenches parallel to the front to afford protection during an artillery barrage. The men usually remained standing, with an NCO in charge, ready for action as soon as the shelling ceased.

Special Purpose Trenches

Telephone lines for general contact between the front and rear areas were laid in trenches and were often fixed to the trench walls. Unfortunately they were very exposed and easily broken by both enemy fire and careless soldiers. Important telephone lines were buried, often in triplicate, in 'trenches' six feet deep, which were then backfilled to bury and hopefully safeguard the lines. See Chapter 8 for more on this subject.

Strongpoints

See Keep.

Sump

A pit dug below duckboards to collect excessive rainwater so that it could be drained or pumped away.

Support Trenches

Similar in design and strength to the front-line trenches, to which they were linked by numerous communication trenches, to facilitate rapid reinforcement. They were sited around 100 yards behind the front and often incorporated some dugouts to offer shelter to soldiers during an artillery bombardment.

Traverse

A traverse was an integral part of the trench that gave it that castellated appearance when seen from above. They were designed to protect against enfilade fire sweeping the length of the trench and to minimize the blast damage from a shell exploding in it. They also gave protection and afforded some ability to recapture a section of trench that might be occupied by the enemy. For this reason loopholes were often cut into the sides of traverses. The distance between traverses ranged from 13 to 20 feet – centre to centre. The techniques for regaining a partially captured trench demanded that the distance must be close enough to throw a grenade into the next traverse but one.

Trench Block

Sometimes the same line of trench was occupied by both sides. This usually occurred during an attack. To stop infiltration along the trench it was blocked, by defender or attacker, with whatever was to hand. If there was a predictable risk of invasion preconstructed barriers of barbed wire in frames were set ready for rapid deployment. Often two blocks, several yards apart, were deployed for better defence.

Chapter 5

A SOLDIER'S LIFE: WHAT IT WAS LIKE

A Summary

Soldiers of the Great War suffered immense hardships with considerable fortitude and yet life was not intolerable all the time. They shared considerable 'black' humour. And the camaraderie was inescapable. It has often been said that men fought for the honour of their regiment. Whilst that is true, I suggest the soldiers' greatest loyalty was to their chums. One must also realize that they were certainly not in battle all or even most of the time. Anywhere in the fighting zones was risky but the most dangerous areas at the front were occupied in rotation. Life was a mixture of hard work, discomfort, boredom – and at times sheer terror. But there were many lighter moments when the soldiers, out of the line, were able to relax to a certain degree. There was always kit to be cleaned, heavy loads to be manhandled, trenches to be dug, rations carried to the front and many other hard jobs that required seemingly limitless manpower. And when all that was done route marches were devised to keep the men fit, occupied and out of mischief. But there was still some time left. Often this was occupied with sleeping. All soldiers quickly learn the knack of being able to sleep anywhere and at anytime – even if only for a very few minutes. Football matches were played. Improvised and infrequent baths were taken. Uniforms were disinfected in a vain attempt to kill the lice infesting them. When freed from duties remaining precious moments were often occupied reading those, so very important, letters from home and sharing with their mates the contents of parcels.

Gambling, in the form of the banned, but still practised, dice game of Crown & Anchor happened surreptitiously. Items that we now treasure in the shape of trench art were crafted. And millions of cigarettes were smoked. The war was not particularly discussed, for the average soldier knew little of what was happening, except in his current area. There was little point in talking about the dangers and discomforts, for his chums had exactly the same experiences. When he went home he did not discuss it there either for his folks could not really appreciate all he went through and the horrors he saw. Consequently the soldier of the Great War grew used to keeping his true feelings to himself. That is the main reason most veterans never really talked to others about the reality of war. They were generally happy to chat about the lighter moments – especially when humour was involved – but one really had to get to know them very well for the truth to gradually emerge about the darker moments. Post-traumatic stress disorder had not been recognized and counselling was non-existent. Soldiers either bottled up their feelings and coped with life or, in the worst cases, committed suicide. Some were eventually incarcerated in mental institutions, perhaps for the rest of their lives. The overall morale of the British forces was however very good, unlike the French and Russians in 1917 and the Germans in 1918.

Infantry and its Specialists

By far the greatest number of men served in the infantry. They were the foot soldiers and the backbone of the army. Their role was to fight the war by denying the enemy access to any more territory than he had already conquered and to seize that back at the first opportunity. In this, artillery, engineers, tanks, machine guns, supply units and other specialists assisted them. But none of these could fulfil the role of the infantry. It required armed men on the ground to take and hold on to territory.

Besides manning the trenches, whilst largely armed with rifles, the infantry gradually developed many other skills. Some became snipers; others light machine gunners. Many operated trench mortars or learnt the expertise of the bomber or grenadier. Their roles were far-reaching and vital. It was men of the infantry who dug most of the trenches and laboured for the tunnellers, road builders, etc. They conveyed their own messages, cooked their own food and buried their own dead. They were truly multi-functional.

There were many elements to life in the trenches and some are examined here.

Getting to the Front

As we have seen, soldiers of the Great War were largely pedestrians. British battalions, moving long distances on the Western Front, were sometimes loaded into French railway boxcars for expediency – although they did travel rather slowly. The carriage was hardly luxurious, being originally designed mainly for horse transport. Indeed the wagons were prominently labelled *Homme 40. Chevaux 8* (Men 40. Horses 8). For added comfort the bare wooden floors were thinly covered in straw. Upon reaching the railhead, they detrained and marched into action. The same principle applied to most armies. There are instances of German soldiers marching 1,000 kilometres in thirty days in 1914! In an attempt to avoid serious blistering of the feet men smeared them with wet soap. The hard pavé (cobbled) roads were especially punishing and most uncomfortable to march on. Many roads were unsurfaced and either very dusty or very muddy, depending upon the weather, after the tramp of many hundreds of boots.

At times of need, buses or lorries might be pressed into service, but that was a rare event. For those interested, a famously preserved London bus 'Ole Bill' can be seen in the Imperial War Museum.

The alternative transport to marching. A French boxcar designed to accommodate 40 soldiers or 8 horses.

Kit

When in action it was common for certain items such as the greatcoat to be left in the large pack with the transport. The downside was that additional ammunition, grenades and trench paraphernalia – such as picks, shovels, sandbags, duckboards, etc. more than made up for the weight of kit left behind. The soldier went into the line, in uniform, with a waterproof cape and such extra items of clothing as could be found to keep him warm. Steel helmets were worn in the fighting areas once they became plentiful in early 1916 and the respirator, once introduced, was always carried.

Besides their weapons to fight with, the British soldiers used over 10 million spades and 5 million pickaxes to dig up much of Northern France. To keep them fed and watered over 17 million mess tins and 12 million water bottles were issued. And to keep warm they were supplied with over 41 million blankets and 15 million ground sheets. Any losses of official kit had to be accounted for and, if it was judged the man had been careless, a stoppage of pay was made. Whilst in the trenches it was almost impossible to keep body and clothing clean. For obvious reasons weapons received the first priority when it came to cleaning. Once out of the line the kit was soon spruced up.

Battles and Trench Raids

Aggression was British policy and is typically illustrated by the Scots Guards history:

> A mere passive defence of these lines was never contemplated. The Germans were to be perpetually harassed, their men killed and their nerves kept on edge by local raids. To facilitate these, lanes were cut in the enemy's wire at intervals by the artillery, and once cut were kept open and unrepaired by regular artillery and machine-gun fire. Into which of these open sores and on what day or what hour, the poison might be injected in the form of a British raid, the Germans could never tell. (Petre et al., *Scots Guards in the Great War* (1925), p. 129)

By this aggressive stance it might appear that soldiers were always fighting. In reality there were far more periods of inaction than action. It is true there was hostility but it was not everywhere nor for every soldier. There were several 'quiet' sectors on the Western Front. And some units were more belligerent than others. The more successful divisions were sent into the fray more often than those judged inefficient, which is why some battalions saw more than their fair share of fighting.

Action was infinitely variable in its nature. It could be by day or night; in large formations or small patrols. Despite discarding certain items, the soldier usually carried over 46lbs of basic kit into action. To this was added extra ammunition and tools. He was truly a human packhorse expected to fight for his life on reaching his destination. No wonder men walked, rather than ran, into action. They had to climb from their own trench; traverse gaps cut in their own barbed wire; cross No Man's Land strewn with the detritus of war; hack through the enemy's forests of barbed wire and get into the enemy trench systems. All this time they were being shelled, shot at, bombed, burnt or gassed. The stench, crescendo and horrors of battle are indescribable. On arrival they then had to kill or be killed, using any means and any weapons available. Reality was often not as clear-cut as the battle plans, maps and orders envisaged and confusion often reigned. Direction was sometimes lost and Allied units occasionally fought and killed each other in error. And all this for perhaps as little as one shilling and one (old) pence war zone pay a day (less than 6 pence). He could however buy quite a lot with this and he had no real living costs, for the army provided his food, clothing and accommodation.

A veteran gave a most descriptive account of going into action:

> And over the top we'd go. As soon as you got over the top the fear left you; now it's terror. You don't look; you see. You don't hear; you listen. Your nose is filled with fumes and death. You taste the top of your mouth. Your weapon and you are one.

Artillery Formation

This method of deploying soldiers is often used but rarely explained. It evolved for use in offensives. The idea was that the men would not be bunched together in large formations and vulnerable to artillery or machine-gun fire. Essentially it was a number of small columns at varying intervals and distances scattered over the front across which the advance was to be made. The battalion would attack with two companies split across its front of around 400 yards. The other two companies were usually held in support or reserve. The leading companies were divided into half platoons of thirty men at most and arranged unevenly in depth, with perhaps 250 yards between the leading and supporting half platoon.

Rotation from Front to Rear

The amount of time spent in the trenches varied enormously and depended upon the part of the line occupied, the weather, the quality of the unit, the casualties sustained and whether or not relief was possible for one reason or other. In theory the average was about four days in the front-line, followed by another four days in close support. The men then went into reserve – not too far away. Often this was followed by a period in rear areas but sometimes the whole rotation process was repeated with more spells in the trenches. When relief was not possible, much longer periods could be spent at the front. Overall the average infantryman would have spent about half his life in one of the various trench lines – most often back from the front.

A division was assigned a section of the front ranging, on average, from 2,000 to 4,000 yards. Its time spent on duty varied enormously from a few weeks to over one year! It was frequently moved from one area to another. That did not mean however that the men were continuously in the front-line, for there were many to share those duties. The three brigades within a divisional front regularly exchanged from front-lines, to reserve lines, to the rear. Within each brigade of four battalions, two were at or near the front and two in reserve. The four companies of each battalion rotated between the front and support lines. Thus, at any one time, it could be that the actual front-line of the entire division was being held by two companies of less than 500 men. Naturally they could be rapidly reinforced by other units in close support and reserve.

When a new unit took over the line, great care was taken that the enemy should not realize it, otherwise extra shelling and perhaps trench raids might occur to catch them out. It was an ideal time, for the departing troops might relax their guard and the newcomers were not yet aware of all the pitfalls that awaited them. Noise was kept to a minimum and extra sentries were posted. Before the handover, reconnaissance parties consisting of officers and NCOs would examine the trenches and check on trench stores. Junior officers in particular had to keep detailed inventories of many items deposited at the front and report losses and ensure replacement equipment was ordered. The paperwork and questions about missing paraphernalia by brigade staff officers was legion and irksome.

Trench Life

This assumed a rather dull routine, assuming no excessive enemy activity.

It was a troglodyte existence with major activities always taking place at night. The ever-present sniper sought any target and anything appearing above, or in gaps, in the parapet could expect to be shot. Shortly before dawn each day 'Stand-To [your Arms]' was called and all men were ready for immediate action, with bayonets fixed, whilst the enemy lines were examined (by periscopes) for signs of aggression. Snipers crawled into their concealed positions ready for another day's 'bag'. After full daylight, and assuming all was quiet, the order 'Stand-Down' signalled the start of another supposedly normal day. Sentries were posted to peer through their periscopes and immediately sound the alarm if there was any enemy activity.

During daylight hours weapons were cleaned, meals eaten and, after clearing up as much as possible and passing various inspections, most tried to sleep anywhere they could. Breakfast was cooked and tea made in a small trench fireplace. Smoke was kept to a minimum for fear of attracting the attention of the enemy. However aggression was often kept to a minimum at this time of day, for both sides wanted their breakfast in peace and not blown apart. Washing and shaving, if attempted, was done with a little tea kept back for the purpose.

Whether asleep or awake men had to be fully dressed with their equipment on and rifles loaded and immediately to hand. Officers and NCOs regularly visited to ensure procedures and orders were followed. Sentries were posted to listen and watch for signs of enemy activity – including the approach of gas, for which a warning gong (often a hanging shell case) was available. Officers would censor the men's letters home and request any trench stores for delivery that night. Movement of any kind was kept to a minimum. Men wrote letters home, gambled and some made trench art. They also 'chatted' – that is, inspected their uniforms for lice. A candle flame was passed carefully along seams in clothing to expel the insects, which were then crushed between thumbnails. Unfortunately many of these creatures escaped detection to lay more eggs and start a new generation of irritation. Even freshly laundered uniforms quickly became reinfested with lice, which besides causing intense itching, sometimes started sores that easily infected in the unsanitary conditions of trench life. Flies too were a menace. With so much decaying matter in abundance they bred prolifically and contributed to the general unpleasantness. However, by far the most overwhelming condition to be endured in the trench was boredom.

Typical trench scene during daylight hours. Sentry on duty whilst chums sleep. Border Regt in front-line Thiepval Wood, Aug. 1916.

Before dusk 'Stand-To' was again called with similar precautions as at daybreak, before nocturnal activities commenced. Sentries in the fire-bays were posted but this time they stood on the fire-step with head and shoulders exposed above the parapet. A chum was immediately at hand to help if needed, whilst typically the third man in the bay rested. They exchanged tasks regularly. It would not have been possible to observe adequately at night with the periscopes available. By exposing the upper torso there was a chance at least that, if the parapet was swept by predetermined machine-gun fire, a hit might be to the shoulders (at parapet level) rather than in the head!

Nightly activities included: repairs of, or additions to, the wire or parapet; digging of new trenches or saps; reconnaissance or offensive expeditions into No Man's Land; ration parties to and from the rear; the burial of bodies in nearby cemeteries or convenient shell holes; emptying urine pails, digging, refilling or cleaning of latrines; evacuation of wounded; and exchange of front-line units. Padres, medical officers and senior officers made their visits and inspections to offer respectively: comfort, aid, unwanted advice and orders. They could offer little of value that an experienced NCO did not already know. Throughout the night there was much to be done and little time for rest or boredom.

Letters and Parcels

The Army Postal Service, part of the Royal Engineers, was extremely efficient and each day vast numbers of letters and parcels were delivered to and from the Front. Indeed it is estimated that the Home Depot of the service handled two billion letters and 114 million parcels. It was correctly judged that communication with friends and family at home greatly improved the morale of serving soldiers, sailors and airmen. Parcels often contained foodstuffs, such as homemade cakes, not available to the men in France. Other treasured items were warm items of clothing. Whereas letters addressed to a deceased soldier were returned, that did not apply to parcels, which were shared by his chums. Letters were censored for the men, whilst officers were privileged to 'censor' their own mail. Early in the war even place names on picture postcards were obliterated, although what that achieved is difficult to tell. Ordinary soldiers rarely knew anything of military significance and it was largely a pointless task for the junior officers involved. The infrequently distributed 'green envelope' was much sought after by soldiers, for letters enclosed in it were only subjected to censorship at the base and not locally. The owner, however, had to certify that the contents 'refer to nothing but private and family matters'.

For Christmas 1914 Princess Mary, the King's only daughter, organized a fund to supply comforts to everyone in the armed forces. It consisted of a brass box bearing her royal cipher, the names of several countries and the

Princess Mary tin with typical contents.

words 'Christmas 1914'. Besides a Christmas card and picture of the Princess it usually contained a combination of cigarettes and tobacco plus a tinder-lighter. Sometimes a pipe was sent as well. For non-smokers and Indian soldiers sweets, spices or writing material was provided. After consuming the contents many tins were sent home as souvenirs and are quite commonly found today.

Rations

Food was a very important part of a soldier's life. The British soldier was adequately if not extravagantly fed. At least he was most of the time, but there were many occasions in the line when it was not possible for food to be brought to him. To guard against this very real possibility two days rations were taken into the line at each changeover.

When possible hot food was provided from field cookers – a small cart that could prepare enough hot meals for 250 men. At least the food was hot once. But by the time it had been carried, maybe a mile or more, over rough ground at night, I suspect the stew or whatever was at best tepid. As an alternative, basic foodstuffs were often brought to the front-line during the night by ration parties. This would generally consist of loaves of bread, jam, cheese and bacon. It was usually carried to the front in sandbags. The food was not wrapped and in consequence the cheese and bacon was usually quite hairy from the sacking and the bread rather resembled the mud it was frequently dropped in en route. Soldiers were used to this and after grumbling – more about any delay in supply, rather than extra texturing to the food – proceeded to eat it. Improvisation was the order of the day. The bacon was cooked on tiny stoves fuelled by special solid pellets or charcoal, or candle wax or any wood or other fuel scrounged locally. For example, in 1916 around 100,000 Ayrton fans were supplied in the fond hope that by wafting them they could dispel approaching gas clouds. They were useless for the intended purpose but, as the handles were wooden, they provided much needed fuel! Corned beef and army biscuits were also available but not much relished. The canned beef was monotonous and the biscuits extremely hard. A slightly more palatable alternative was Maconachie's tinned ration of meat and vegetables, commonly called 'M and V'. The Ticklers jam supplied was most often made from plums and apples – both plentiful in besieged Britain.

Water carts with heavy galvanized mugs chained to them were located in

Field kitchen 1914.

strategic places in rear areas for thirsty soldiers to grab a quick drink as they passed by. Water for the front-line was usually carried up in former petrol tins. They were washed out prior to use as water carriers but nevertheless petrol had already seeped into the cans' seams and forever tainted the water. In addition to its unpleasant taste it could have a detrimental effect upon the bowels!

The prescribed daily ration initially was:

1¼lb (later reduced to 1lb) fresh meat or 1lb processed meat (corned or bully beef)

1¼lb bread or 1lb biscuit (army biscuits) or 1lb flour
4 oz bacon
3 oz cheese
2 oz peas or beans or dried potatoes
Small measures of jam, sugar, salt, mustard, pepper and lime juice
Up to 2oz tobacco and ½ gill (71ml) rum could be discretionally supplied

A brief comparison of just three items of field rations between British, German and American troops is rather interesting, if not surprising (see Table 4). Each number is the daily ration in ounces. Those at home and on lines of communication (except Americans) received less, especially meat and bread. They were the official figures. Frequently because of enemy action, or theft in the supply chain, the men at the front received far less than their full ration.

Table 4. Comparison of three items of field rations			
Item	Britain	America	Germany
Bread	16 oz	16 oz	26.4 oz
Meat	16 oz	20 oz	10.5 oz
Vegetables	10 oz	20 oz	18 oz
Calories per day	4,193	4,714	4,038

Many civilians received an average of not much more than 3,000 calories a day. That may sound good but one must remember that most were working long hours of hard manual labour. The composition of the food at home was filling but not particularly nutritious.

Weight Guide
16 oz (ounce) = 1lb (one pound)
1lb (pound) = .453 kilo or about ½ kilo.
Thus one kilo equals 2.2lbs and 1 ounce equals 28.34 grams.

Iron rations were defined in 1914 as consisting of: one pound of preserved meat (bully beef); three-quarters of a pound of (army) biscuit, approximately quarter pound cheese and half an ounce of tea, plus sugar, salt and meat extract (Bovril). The army biscuit was constructed to confound human teeth and only breakable by force; often an entrenching tool handle was used to knock pieces off. (Perhaps that is why they were called 'iron rations'!) Some were made by Huntley Palmer and endorsed 'Army No. 4'. Others were manufactured by the Delhi Biscuit Company. No doubt other contractors baked the unpalatable item as well. I understand the recipe for army biscuits is the same as that currently used by a well-known manufacturer of dog biscuits. An officer's permission was normally required before the iron rations could be consumed.

Pay

The men were paid in the local currency (French or Belgian francs on the Western Front) at irregular pay parades when out of the line. Indeed, the instructions stated that issues of pay 'will not be made more often than is necessary'. Soldiers had to formally and smartly queue up in front of an officer, salute, produce their pay book for it to be endorsed by the officer with the amount paid and then be dismissed in true military fashion. All payments made were recorded on the acquittance rolls, which had to be promptly forwarded to the regimental paymaster at the base. The paying officer was personally held responsible for any discrepancies.

Battle Hardening

It really is amazing how quickly the men became accustomed to the most frightful sights, sounds and smells imaginable. The overpowering stench of death from unburied human and animal bodies surely pervaded the entire war zone. The noise of explosions not only shattered eardrums but rocked brains within their skulls, inflicting untold damage. And as for the sights of mangled bodies on an almost daily basis, it really does make one wonder how men coped and remained sane. It took just two weeks for the novice soldier to become so accustomed to death that he scarcely gave it another thought. Even the death of a best mate was seen as inevitable and to be avenged if possible, rather than mourned. There was so much carnage there was no time for pity. It is no wonder the men smoked so much. The only concern was availability (cigarettes were often supplied and additional ones were quite cheap – Woodbines 3d for twenty) and how to light them. Matches were hard to find and keep dry so lighters or tinder-lighters prevailed. The rum ration – if approved by the officer commanding, and not stolen en route – was eagerly awaited. The letters SRD stamped on rum jars officially stood for 'Special Ration Department', but the cynical soldiers soon dubbed the letters 'Seldom Reaches Destination'.

Despite the huge casualty lists few veterans ever admitted to deliberately killing enemy soldiers. Of course there are plentiful such accounts in literature but when critically examined, and the numbers totalled up, they really do not amount to very many deaths. This is partly because by far the greatest number of deaths occurred at a distance from the effects of shellfire. Most infantrymen fired their rifles in the general direction of the enemy at times but few, apart from snipers, took deliberate aim at a single man and then killed him. Machine gunners probably took the greatest toll with bullets, at the relatively short range of say 1,000 yards. But at that distance human features cannot really be recognized. Hand-to-hand fighting with bayonets, guns, coshes, etc., certainly occurred, however the resulting deaths were comparatively few compared to the overall carnage. There are nevertheless several accounts of aggression where retribution was the driving force. Men who had suffered at the hands of a particular unit or category of the enemy, such as a sniper, machine-gunner or mortar-man, showed little mercy if they encountered one. Surrender, if offered, was frequently refused and the unfortunate victim summarily despatched – usually by being run through with a bayonet.

As well as being hardened to the elements of battle, the other element soldiers had to endure was the weather. Their uniforms were not waterproof and were not adequately warm in the extremes of winters such as 1916/17. A rather smelly goatskin fleece or leather jerkin was issued for cold weather but it was scarcely adequate. Other garments were sent from home or improvised and at times the nationality of the soldier was difficult to determine from his garb. An issue cape was waterproof but only kept the worst off. Water still dripped down the neck. It also seeped through or over the leather boots. In summer the heat of the woollen uniform made it rather uncomfortable. The soldier of the Great War was certainly a tough individual.

Discipline

This was strictly enforced throughout the war and backed up by the severest penalties for transgressions. Whilst soldiers did not salute officers in the trenches there was no fraternization either. Once away from the front, the full pomp of military life resumed and differed little from that in barracks and parade squares back home. Altogether 304,262 officers and men appeared before a court martial during the war. When one considers that represents just over 3 per cent of the total mobilized from Britain and the Commonwealth, the discipline record of the army is extremely good. Not all those charged were found guilty of course. Whereas imprisonment, usually with hard labour, was an option for courts martial, it was more usual for fines to be imposed for minor offences and Field Punishments No. 1 or 2 for more serious matters. These involved, for No. 2, being physically restricted in shackles and, for No. 1, additionally chained uncomfortably to a fixed object, such as a wagon wheel, for two hours a day. This could continue for three out of every four days – maybe for between three weeks and three months. When not restricted the man was subjected to hard labour and loss of pay and privileges. In total 80,969 sentences to Field Punishment No. 1 or 2 were passed.

The most severe crimes were subject to the death penalty and this is discussed elsewhere. Officers were subject to the same discipline but it seems to have been applied less vigorously. Some 1,085 officers were dismissed from the Army. That is not altogether a soft option for they could then be conscripted as private soldiers.

Desertion

Despite the potentially severe punishments, including execution, that could be handed down there were 114,670 instances of desertion from the Army. Many rejoined; some deserted more than once; 266 paid the ultimate penalty. No doubt some got completely away to lead a secret life as a fugitive.

Billets

When away from the trenches, soldiers were housed in whatever accommodation could be found. Often barns and other farm buildings were commandeered (and paid for) by the Army and the men bedded down on straw if they were lucky. Occasionally better quarters were available. Officers generally found houses to requisition and sleep in. When away from the front the food improved considerably with the availability of the company cookers. More elaborate cleaning of the body, weapons, ammunition and kit was undertaken. A favourite place for soldiers' baths was the local brewery where old vats were commandeered. Water was heated (if they were lucky) and as many men as possible piled in at once. Despite the gradual solidification of the water, the grubby soldiers genuinely relished the opportunity to bathe. Whilst they were naked, sometimes to the glee of the local girls, their uniforms were disinfected and fresh underclothes were issued – very often of a totally different size to the ones removed. And finally, when all this was done, new tasks were found to keep the soldier busy.

Estaminets

These were usually small cafes or bars in rear areas still being run by local French and Belgian families. The usual bill of fare was coffee, cheap beer or the famous 'van blank' (*vin blanc*). The most popular food seems to have been 'oof and frits' (*œuf et frites* – egg and chips). And occasionally the proprietor's daughter became very friendly with visiting soldiers. Whenever possible off-duty soldiers tried to get to the nearest estaminet for some light relief.

Writing paper, cigarettes, tobacco, chocolate and other sundries were often purchased from huts run by organizations such as the Salvation Army, YMCA and similar bodies.

Religious Services and Padres

Services were held if possible in rear areas away from the fighting by Church of England, Roman Catholic, Jewish, Presbyterian, Baptist, Methodist and other ministers of religious faiths. Drumhead services were sometimes held on the eve of battle close to the front. Chaplains to the forces, within the Royal Army Chaplain's Department, were appointed in various classes from I to IV, which ranked from colonel to captain. They visited sick and wounded soldiers and conducted burial services if possible. Many visited the soldiers in the trenches, although soldiers usually complained that chaplains rarely if ever came to dangerous areas. That does not quite tally with the fact that three were awarded the Victoria Cross and 163 died, or were killed, in the course of their ministry during the Great War.

Prisoners of War

Aside from the very real risk of being killed or wounded there was a possibility of being captured by the enemy and made a prisoner for the duration of the war. It was often difficult to surrender alive but once the surrender had been recognized most prisoners were well treated. Many were malnourished but that was mainly because of the scarcity of food in Germany. Some severely wounded men were repatriated home via the Red Cross in Switzerland, but for the others the length of their confinement was unknown. Officers were required, upon repatriation, to justify their capture. In total some 6,949 British officers and 166,626 other ranks (this includes officers and men from the Royal Navy) were reported as having been prisoners of war or interned in neutral countries. Altogether 196,318 Commonwealth officers and men were captured and of these 16,402 died in captivity.

Leaving the Army – Honourably and Alive!

Although men in Kitchener's Armies were technically regular soldiers, their duration of service was effectively for the duration of the war. Because of the requirements of the Army of Occupation of the Rhine, regarrisoning the Empire with regular soldiers and fighting in Russia, etc., some men were retained. Additionally it was not possible for literally millions of men to leave simultaneously. Some men had already left to return to vital war work. Those with jobs waiting got some priority and there was a programme of release for the others. It was not however perceived as entirely fair and a certain amount of unrest occurred from soldiers awaiting release long after the end of the war. Regular soldiers naturally remained in the army. Territorial Force men, once released from active service, resumed their civilian roles, interspersed with military training and camps.

Various procedures, including the following, were carried out at Dispersal Stations:

- A medical examination recorded any injuries that might result in compensation.
- An inventory of equipment was taken. Deficiencies usually had to be paid for.
- Any remaining foreign currency was exchanged for sterling.
- Final pay and war gratuity was calculated and eventually paid.

Many Army Forms (AF) were completed, and some given to the soldier. Only a few can be described here.

- AF Z.11 was a protection certificate: a form identifying the soldier, authorizing an advance of £2 against monies due, and providing for more pay in instalments whilst on the 28 days furlough (leave).
- AF B.108E was a character certificate and vital for his next employment: with so many men looking for work, employers could afford to be choosy. It also certified the length of service in the Army.
- AF Z.21, perhaps the most important form, was the one that authorized his immediate future on leaving the Army.

There were four categories of release.

- Discharge (final release from the Army)
- Transfer to various classes of reserve.
- Disembodiment: the terminology used when a member of the Territorial Force is released from full-time active service.
- Demobilization: date physically left the army, but not necessarily without conditions, such as reserve service.

It also gave some medal entitlement details and of where to rejoin if recalled. Reserve classes were:

Classes P, T and W	Authority to leave the forces and return to civilian duties. duties. It mostly applied to vital war work. Each class varies slightly in the conditions attached to the soldier's release.
Class Z	The most common. Most soldiers were not finally discharged at the end of 1918 but transferred to Class Z Reserve. This was in case Germany rejected the peace conditions and resumed hostilities. By March 1920 most men were finally released from the army.

Some received slips certifying such matters as that they were 'free from vermin, scabies and venereal disease'; and 'that clothing, boots etc are in a clean and serviceable condition'. The soldier could keep his steel helmet, boots and uniform but was not supposed to wear it with any badges or insignia after twenty-eight days. His greatcoat could be kept or exchanged for one pound. He was additionally given a ration book, an unemployment insurance policy, a railway warrant for travel home and civilian clothing.

Sailors who were killed or died in service were recorded as 'discharged dead'.

Chapter 6

WEAPONS OF WAR

Introduction

All 'guns', using the word generically, and no matter whether pistol, rifle, machine gun, mortar or artillery piece, have similar methods of operation and fulfil similar roles to a greater or lesser degree. Each normally uses a chemical propellant, effectively a relatively slow-burning explosive, to drive a projectile towards its target.

18-pounder field gun in action

Originally, guns fired mostly spherical objects through a smooth-bored barrel. The accuracy was greatly enhanced by rifling – a series of spiral groves cut into the inside (the bore) of a gun barrel – which caused the bullet or shell to spin. The gyroscopic effect created improved range and accuracy considerably, as the projectile remained point first and thus streamlined. Many rifling groves have a right-hand twist but the British SMLE rifles and Vickers machine guns, along with some French weapons, have a left-hand twist. This can easily be seen impressed on fired bullets. The copper (driving) bands on fired artillery shells will be seen to have been scored by the rifling as well. If a bullet or shell does not bear indications of rifling then it probably has never been fired. If the driving band on a shell has been removed, then it is often difficult to tell whether or not it has been fired.

In this section a brief description of the most important guns and types of guns will give an idea of the basic operation of the many hundreds of variations employed by the belligerent nations.

All small arms, machine guns and the lighter artillery pieces use a self-contained 'round of ammunition'. This usually consists of a brass (or alternative material) cartridge case, containing in its base a primer that, on being struck by a firing pin, explodes and sends a jet of flame into the cartridge case. Inside the cartridge case is a compound of propellant such as cordite or nitrocellulose that is lit by the primer. Pressure builds up and forces the bullet or shell out of the neck of the case into the barrel of the gun and onwards towards its target. The bullet or shell may be solid or may contain various materials depending on the space available and its purpose. The round of ammunition is initially placed, ready for firing, into the base or 'breech' of the barrel. That is a slightly wider and stronger area built to contain the complete cartridge case. In small arms the term used is 'chamber'.

The term 'small arms' applies to the weapons usually carried by a soldier, such as a pistol, rifle or light machine gun. They were cleaned regularly to try to ensure they would fire when required. Oil was kept in a small brass tube in a hollow in the butt of the rifle along with a cord, weighted at one end and known as a 'pull-through'. A small piece of flannelette, measuring four by two inches, was inserted in a loop in the cord, lubricated with oil, and pulled through the bore of the gun to remove fouling that could cause rust. The flannelette was supplied in rolls and strips torn off it as required. During the war enough length of flannelette was supplied to more than circle the earth at the equator. There are numerous excellent specialist books detailing specific guns, from pistols to the largest artillery pieces, which may be consulted if required.

Rifles and Bayonets

The rifle was the personal weapon, and most important piece of kit, of most soldiers in the First World War. It was cherished or hated but nevertheless cleaned and inspected regularly. Many different rifles or pattern of rifles were in use by the belligerent nations throughout the 1914–18 war. Shorter rifles, some intended for use by the cavalry, were called carbines. Here we only briefly consider two of the most famous rifles.

British Rifle

The standard service rifle of the Great War was the Short, Magazine, Lee-Enfield or 'SMLE' as it was known. The name came about because the rifle was shorter than earlier versions and it had a magazine for cartridges; James Lee invented the rear-locking bolt system; and it was initially made at the Royal Small Arms Factory at Enfield, Middlesex. Later, several wartime contractors, both at home and abroad, manufactured it. Various marks of the rifle evolved but the most common during the Great War were the Mark III and Mark III* which simplified the earlier version. The weight of the SMLE was 8lbs 10oz (4kg), unloaded and without a bayonet.

The rifle's magazine held ten cartridges, otherwise known as 'rounds'. They were loaded into it from above, using disposable clips which each held five cartridges. The rifle used a bolt-action system. To shoot, each round had to be fed into the part of the barrel, known as the chamber, by using the bolt. It was opened and closed in a somewhat similar fashion to a common door bolt. As the bolt was lifted, thus unlocking it and then pulled to the rear, any previously fired cartridge was ejected. Simultaneously a fresh cartridge was pushed up by a spring from the magazine beneath it. The bolt was then pushed forward, feeding that cartridge into the chamber. Finally, and before the rifle could be fired, the bolt was pushed down to lock it safely into place. The rifle was aimed and its trigger squeezed. After each shot was fired the above procedure had to be repeated. The pre-war British infantry soldier was trained to fire his rifle at the rate of fifteen accurate shots per minute. This endeavour entailed reloading the magazine that only held ten rounds. Such a sustained high rate of rifle fire gave rise to the German belief that we had far more machine guns than was the case in the early days of the war. Unfortunately the high standard of marksmanship was unable to be maintained during accelerated wartime training. An average of perhaps eight rounds per minute for rapid fire would be more realistic.

The standard British rifle cartridge of the time was of .303 calibre and had evolved into the Mark VII. The 174-grain spitzer (i.e. pointed, as opposed to round-nosed) bullet had a muzzle velocity of 2,440ft/sec. that delivered 2,408ft/lb energy at the muzzle. For its time it was a highly efficient cartridge in all aspects. And, according to Ordnance Committee calculations, should the rifle be elevated to nearly 35 degrees, the bullet was theoretically capable of travelling 4,457 yards (4,075m) before it would fall to the ground some 31 seconds later. They said that, even at that distance, it would be travelling at 416ft/sec and capable of inflicting serious injury. In fact it took just one second to travel the first 600 yards (548m) – the velocity decaying rapidly the further it travelled. For practical purposes 1,000 yards was considered its reasonable maximum range, although in reality most aimed shots were at considerably less distance than that. After all, if one cannot see the target one can hardly be expected to hit it! That said, the SMLE was sighted to 2,000 yards and the Vickers machine gun to 2,900 yards, so very long-range shooting had at least been contemplated when these weapons were designed. Hundreds of millions of rounds were fired during the war but we still had over 325 million .303 cartridges left by November 1918.

Incendiary ammunition was developed for use against Zeppelins and other specialist ammunition was introduced to fill particular requirements.

British Bayonet

The SMLE accepts a sword bayonet Pattern 1907 that has a blade length of seventeen inches, wooden grips and weighs, with scabbard, over one and a half pounds (750g). It was attached to a circular protuberance just below the muzzle of the rifle and clipped into place on a lug beneath the barrel. The scabbard in particular was simplified to meet wartime production quotas and the bayonet itself was soon made without an upturned hook to its quillon (cross-guard) that was regarded as unnecessary.

German Rifle

The standard rifle of the Great War was the Mauser Gewehr (rifle) 98. It had a calibre of 7.92mm and overall its operation, size and performance was roughly similar to the British SMLE. It did however have two major differences. The bolt design, and especially the method of locking it, gave the rifle greater strength and accuracy. The drawback was that its rate of fire and reloading was far slower than the SMLE. Additionally, the magazine of the Mauser G.98 held only five rounds. It was however an extremely good rifle and served not only the German Army but also many others throughout the world.

German Bayonet

The G.98 accepted many different bayonets, some of which were Ersatz models, made wholly from steel to economize on other materials and simplify production. The most famous German bayonet was by far the so-called 'butcher's knife', for that is what it closely resembled. Here again there were several variations but the one that caused most concern and adverse propaganda was the saw-backed version. It was portrayed as barbaric but in reality was used as a dual-purpose item by pioneers and artillerymen. The saw back was intended for cutting wood and not to inflict a jagged wound – although it could no doubt do so if thrust in too deeply.

Pistols

The pistol or handgun was initially almost a badge of office for officers and very few others carried one. Officers had to purchase their own pistol, which could be any make or model but had to accept government ammunition of .455 calibre. Most initially chose the Webley Mk IV revolver but the Webley Mk VI revolver, slowly introduced from mid-1915, gradually became the firm favourite. It held six rounds and, with practice, was capable of accurate shooting to fifty yards or more. Later it was issued to other ranks, at government expense, where deemed necessary – for example, to machine gunners, despatch riders, tank crews, etc., where a rifle would have been unnecessarily cumbersome.

The popular German pistol, seen in films and indeed used extensively throughout the war, was the P'08 Luger in 9mm (parabellum) calibre. That is essentially the same cartridge still used throughout the world in hundreds of different firearms. The P'08 Luger is a semi-automatic pistol holding eight rounds in a detachable magazine that fits inside the grips (handle). As each shot was fired, the empty case was automatically ejected and a fresh round loaded ready to be fired next time the trigger was depressed. The magazine was removed to reload, or it could be replaced by a spare magazine that was already filled. This enabled a faster rate of fire than a revolver that had to be opened by the shooter and the fired cases manually ejected before fresh cartridges were inserted, then the weapon had to be closed ready to resume firing.

Machine Guns

Unlike a rifle or pistol, a machine gun is a firearm capable of continuous fire for as long as the trigger is depressed and the ammunition supply remains available – subject to mechanical failure. Britain and Germany used similar medium machine guns, both based upon the original design of Sir Hiram Maxim, but modified to suit requirements. The two guns performed in a very comparable way. The British version was the Vickers Machine Gun Mk 1 in .303 calibre. When complete, with its essential water for cooling, it weighed over 40lbs. The necessary tripod weighed an additional 52lbs. In total, but without ammunition, 92lbs (42kg) – not easily portable! Medium machine guns were usually sited in very well concealed positions slightly back from, or actually at, the front.

The German gun was the MG '08 in 7.92mm calibre and was usually mounted on a sledge rather than a tripod. Altogether it weighed 137lbs

Vickers machine gun being fired during a gas attack on 2 May 1915 by John Lynn VC, DCM. He died the same day from gas poisoning.

(62kg). Both countries' guns fired at the rate of around 400–500 rounds per minute with the ammunition contained in fabric belts that each held 250 rounds. A team member fed the belts of ammunition into the gun. They were heavy (a box of 250 rounds and belt weighed 22lbs) and did not last long on continuous fire. Most often the guns were fired in short bursts of a few rounds to conserve ammunition stocks and avoid the gun overheating. Instances of 10,000 rounds per hour, sustained fire, are however well documented. In 1915 a lighter version of the German MG '08 was introduced for certain tasks.

The .303 Lewis Machine Gun was introduced into British service in 1915. Of American design, this 'lightweight' gun, at 28lbs (13kg), revolutionized warfare. For the first time it was possible for a single infantryman to carry into action a fully automatic weapon. It was air-cooled, fired at a rate of up to 550 rounds per minute and used a circular magazine holding 47 rounds of ammunition. A full magazine would only last five seconds on continuous fire but firing in short bursts was always more efficient. Naturally the machine gunner had assistants carrying spare magazines of ammunition, but it was no longer necessary to have a large support team for every machine gun. A stripped-down version was made for use in aircraft and the magazine for that held 97 rounds.

Hand Grenades

The use of hand grenades or 'bombs' was well known prior to the First World War. Indeed the Grenadier Guards history dates back to 1656. As the name implies, grenadiers originally specialized in throwing bombs at the enemy. It was not however until the Great War that 'safe' yet easily ignited bombs were developed. And the throwers were by then usually referred to as 'bombers'. Germany started the war better equipped with safer and more reliable bombs than the British. Indeed in the early months of the war, British engineers and troops frequently improvised grenades as existing manufactured stocks became exhausted. Some, known as 'jam-tin bombs', were simply old tins refilled with explosives and scrap iron, then fused ready to be lit and thrown when the opportunity presented itself. Despite many millions of grenades being thrown, the residual British stock in France at the Armistice was over seven million.

Although a multitude of grenades appeared between 1914 and 1918 I will only consider here the two most commonly encountered: one British and one German, and both coming into use in 1915. From very small stockpiles in 1914 all belligerents manufactured very many millions of grenades during the next four years. It became one of the most effective offensive infantry weapons of the war.

British: The Mills Bomb

Introduced as the No. 5 Mk I, it was an egg-shaped device made from thick, segmented cast iron that shattered into fragments when it exploded. The base was sealed with a screw plug that was opened to insert the detonator. The top was shaped to accommodate a striker lever and retaining split pin. It weighed nearly one and a half pounds when filled with explosives and was just under four inches in length. A well-trained man could accurately pitch a Mills Bomb about thirty-five yards. To operate, the bomb was grasped firmly, so as to restrain the striker safety lever, whilst the safety pin was withdrawn. All the time the lever was held against the body of the bomb it would not explode. When thrown (or more properly pitched, rather like a cricket ball) a powerful spring would cause the lever to fly off and simultaneously propel the internal striker into a cap thus starting a timed safety fuse of usually five seconds. When the fuse burned into the main detonator it would explode the bomb. A specialized bomber would carry, in addition to his rifle and other equipment, eighteen Mills bombs in a canvas bucket.

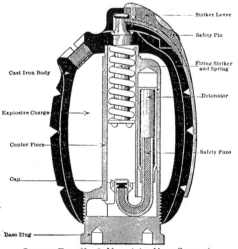

GRENADE HAND NO. 5, MARK 1 (OR MILLS GRENADE).

Section of Mills bomb showing components.

Hand grenade No. 5 Mk 1 (Mills bomb). Terry Whippy Collection.

German: The Stick Grenade

Evolved from the 1915 model, the 1917 version is the one most frequently portrayed in books and films. At nearly double the weight and over three times the length of a British Mills Bomb the German stick grenade was more cumbersome but its very length permitted it to be thrown further than the Mills. The four-inch long cylindrical body of the grenade had a hollow wooden handle screwed to its base. Its popular name of 'potato masher' accurately described the weapon that, with its thin sheet steel body, relied upon explosive force rather than fragmentation for effect. To use, a screw cap was removed from the bottom of the hollow handle thus releasing a ceramic pull ring with a thin cord attached. The other end of the cord was attached to a friction ignition system that, upon pulling, started a time fuse of about six seconds. There was no going back – once the fuse was activated the bomb had to be thrown. Other versions were introduced that automatically 'lit' upon being thrown.

German stick genade. Terry Whippy Collection.

Like most other munitions of war there are many variations of grenades. Their exact measurements, methods of fusing and use differed considerably but the basic principles remained. Each was a small explosive bomb that could be carried relatively safely by a soldier until required. It was then activated and lobbed towards the enemy with varying degrees of success. Some grenades were designed or modified to be fired using rifles or other launchers in order to achieve a greater range. Those interested should refer to specialist publications for precise information.

Artillery

The responsibility of the Royal Artillery in the First World War is discussed in Chapter 8. Here, we are only concerned with the weapons and their projectiles. All artillery pieces fired a projectile, at high speed and with considerable accuracy over a relatively long range. That range far exceeded the capabilities of any small arms, machine guns or mortars. The projectile was a canister capable of containing different contents, the use of which depended upon the job the projectile, normally a shell, was required to do.

The guns themselves, besides differing considerably in size, portability and method of loading, were divided into two main groups. There were guns and there were howitzers. Both guns and howitzers could be large or small. The difference was their design and purpose. The smaller guns were called field guns. A gun was intended for direct fire. That is, the target, even if a long way away, was preferably visible to the gunner or forward observation officer. A howitzer, using variable propellant charges, was intended to fire at a high angle, over an obstacle obscuring the view of the gunner. It will be appreciated there was considerable crossover of use. The above definitions were, in reality, largely theoretical. Often a faraway target had to be fired at by prediction rather than direct observation. Howitzers, when fired at a much lower angle than their maximum capability, behaved in a similar way to guns.

The way the main part of each gun or howitzer (i.e. barrel and breech) was supported varied in two main ways. It could be on wheels or a fixed mounting. Some were so heavy they had to be dismantled to transport over even short distances. After firing a certain number of rounds, the barrel of an artillery piece suffered considerably from erosion and corrosion. It began to wear out. Each shot produced considerable friction between the driving bands of the shell and the rifled barrel. If it and other parts were not replaced regularly, accuracy suffered considerably.

Guns are classified according to their size. The 18-pounder field gun was so named because the shell it fired weighed (notionally) 18lbs. The 9.2" howitzer conversely was so named because that was the diameter of its shell. Great War artillery ranged from 1-pounder, where the shell weighed one pound, to the huge 15" howitzer firing a shell weighing over half a ton. Some German and Austrian shells were far larger still. Despite huge losses of artillery pieces by the war's end, there remained 7,578 British guns and howitzers in France and Belgium, plus nearly sixteen million shells.

The shells for the field guns of the Royal Horse and Royal Field Artillery were self-contained – that is, the propellant charge was contained in a shell case that also held in its neck the projectile (shell). It looked rather like a very large rifle cartridge. The advantage of this system is that the entire round of ammunition was loaded as one unit into the gun. It was fired and the empty case subsequently ejected. With a heavier shell it was not practical to use this method. The shell was first loaded into the breech of the gun and then the propellant, in combustible bags, was inserted behind it.

Assembled 18-pounder shell.

After the gun had fired there was no empty case to eject. Each system, together with the finer points of the guns and ammunition, had advantages and disadvantages, the technical details of which are the subject of specialist publications.

Shells came in two main groupings: high explosive and carrier shells. High explosive shells were used against most targets once trench warfare was established. Depending upon their size and fusing they were capable of damaging or destroying trenches and fortifications. Casualties were caused by the blast effect of the high explosives, collapsing trenches, etc. or simply by being struck by high velocity jagged pieces of shattered shell casing (not to be confused with shrapnel). High explosive rounds were usually fitted with a fuse that detonated the shell on impact.

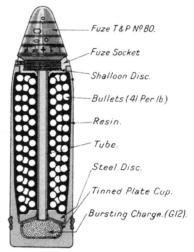

18-pounder shrapnel shell, sectioned to show workings.

Fuze T&P Nº 80.
Fuze Socket
Shalloon Disc.
Bullets (41 Per lb.)
Resin.
Tube.
Steel. Disc.
Tinned Plate Cup.
Bursting Charge. (G12).

The carrier shells could contain many things. In the early months of the war it was invariably shrapnel. Shrapnel is strictly small balls of lead blown from a special shell, after a time interval, whilst the shell is still in the air. They were designed originally to burst over the heads of troops in the open. Later they were used to cut barbed wire with varying degrees of success. The shrapnel balls (often called 'shrapnel bullets') were typically one half-inch diameter, although some were much larger. The 18-pounder shell held 375 such shrapnel balls. Larger calibre shrapnel shells naturally held considerably more balls. Other fillings for carrier shells included incendiary compounds, smoke, illuminating materials and irritant or poison gas. Carrier shells were usually fitted with fuses that caused the shell to discharge its contents after a time interval. The fuse was set to activate the shell by deciding the distance to the target and then calculating the time it would take to go that far.

Table 5. Some of the British Artillery Pieces of the War		
Equipment and its weight	Shell weight	Maximum range
18-pdr (Mk 1) 1.25 tons	18lbs	6,525 yards
4.5" howitzer 1.45 tons	35lbs	7,300 yards
4.7" field gun 3.75 tons	45lbs	10,000 yards
60-pdr (Mk 1) 4.5 tons	60lbs	12,300 yards
6" (26cwt) howitzer 3.63 tons	100lbs	11,400 yards
6" (Mk 19) field gun 10.2 tons	100lbs	18,750 yards
9.2" (Mk 1) howitzer 13.3 tons*	290lbs	10,060 yards
14" rail gun (Mk 3) 248 tons	1,400lbs	34,600 yards
15" howitzer 10.7 tons	1,400lbs	10,795 yards

* A ballast box filled with 9 tons of earth was also required for this howitzer.

Because most shells were supersonic at the muzzle of the gun (speed of sound notionally 1130ft/sec (344m/sec) at sea level), it was common for close-range shots to arrive before the report of the gun that fired them. British soldiers gave the name 'whiz-bang' to this type of German shell. The names 'coal-box' or 'Jack Johnson's' (the latter after a famous American boxer) were attributed to German heavy shells giving off clouds of dense black smoke when bursting.

Mortars

One of the main differences between a gun and a mortar is the cost and simplicity of production of the latter. Fulfilling a similar role to a howitzer, the mortar was designed to 'lob' an explosive projectile over a relatively short range but in a high arc or trajectory so as to clear intervening obstacles. They are primarily muzzle-loading weapons and, in smaller calibres, relatively light and portable. Many, but not all mortars were smooth-bored, again for simplicity. Being relatively small many mortars could be concealed in and fired from trenches whereas this would have been all but impossible for an artillery piece.

In the conditions of the Western Front the mortar was an ideal weapon. Generally the opposing trenches were less than 800 yards apart – most far less than that. With the high arc of the bomb it descended almost vertically and in consequence it was possible to lob a mortar bomb directly into an enemy trench. As long range was not required, the mortar bomb was propelled by a relatively small charge that developed low pressures. In consequence very strong and heavy barrels were not necessary, which all added to the portability of the mortar. With a much smaller propellant charge the pressures on the bomb were also less than on a shell fired by a gun or howitzer. Again, because of this, it was possible to reduce the amount of protective steel surrounding the high explosive bursting charge in the bomb. Overall the ratio of charge to total weight was extremely efficient at up to 40 per cent, as opposed to around 12 per cent, or sometimes much less, explosive in a typical shell fired from an artillery gun or howitzer.

Mortars were much feared by soldiers because of the devastation they caused. However, because of their operation – low velocity and high angle of fire – experienced troops learnt to listen out for the distinctive 'plop' of their being fired. They then scoured the skies for sight of the mortar bomb coming their way and rapidly took evasive action! Infantry soldiers not only disliked enemy mortars, they were not too impressed by our own mortar companies which had a habit of turning up in a trench unannounced, firing off a few bombs and then retreating rapidly from whence they came. The enemy was soon able to calculate the area the assault originated and retaliate in kind, leaving the poor infantry to reap the whirlwind occasioned by the mortar teams.

At the beginning of the war the German (and Austro-Hungarian) Armies had a variety of huge mortars (known in Germany as *Minenwerfer* – literally 'mine-launcher'). The enormous 42cm Mörser, along with the 25cm model and others, was used to destroy the forts in Liège, Namur and Mauberge. Later on came many more designs, notably the light 7.58cm model. All these weapons were highly efficient and yet the French and British really had next

German Minenwerfer *in the act of firing.* Julian Sykes archives.

to nothing to counter them to start with. Even large catapults were tried in desperation.

Experiments with French museum exhibits, relics from earlier conflicts, convinced the British that mortars had a lot to offer. Two models evolved in 1915 after many failed or inefficient prototypes. Officially named Bomb HE 2" Trench Mortar, our first example was a spherical bomb mounted on a two inch steel tubular stave. It was affectionately called either a 'plum pudding' or a 'toffee-apple' by the troops. The bomb weighed altogether 60lbs (27kg) of which 10lbs was the weight of the two inch stave which occasionally, rather alarmingly, came straight back towards the firer! A plum pudding was capable of being fired 500 yards. The large explosive charge of 20lbs of ammonal, lyddite or amatol was quite effective in destroying wire entanglements if the bomb exploded in the correct place. There were however teething problems. The early bombs, with a slow-to-react fuse created a large crater, which gave a false sense of security. It often appeared from a distance that the wire had been cleared when in fact it was hidden, perhaps under water, in the crater. This problem was solved by the introduction of a fuse (no. 107) that detonated the bomb instantaneously, shattered the wire into fragments and formed little or no crater. One of the drawbacks to this weapon was its weight. The bombs were not exactly light at 60lbs, including the stave, and the mortar itself weighed in at 285lbs (130kg), which did not lend itself to rapid portability.

The other stalwart British mortar was the three-inch Stokes. Weighing almost 10lbs (4.5kg) that bomb could travel nearly 1,200 yards (1,100m). It was initially fitted with a modified grenade fuse before an 'always' impact fuse was developed. (It would explode the bomb no matter which way up it landed.) The mortar, from which it was fired, was very simple and reasonably portable, consisting of a metal tube on a base-plate supported by a bi-pod mount. Sights were added for aiming purposes. Bombs could be fired rapidly by simply dropping each one, base first, down the barrel after removing the safety pin. On reaching the bottom of the barrel a striker automatically fired a propellant charge contained within the bomb. Because of its simplicity a rate of fire of twenty-two bombs per minute has been known, with often seven or more being in the air at once from the same mortar!

After initial confusion as to who exactly was responsible for these new weapons a system evolved whereby Infantry Brigades were in charge of light mortars such as the Stokes, and Division Artillery took charge of the heavier equipment. Dedicated trench mortar officers were appointed and personnel had their own identifying badge.

Landmines

Landmines must not be confused with large charges placed at the end of tunnels dug under enemy positions and detonated by the minelayer at a time of his choosing. There is a separate section on that subject in Chapter 8.

A landmine is triggered, usually unintentionally, by its victim. The modern concept of a landmine or anti-tank mine is a device designed and manufactured to be hidden and detonate when trodden on or run over. It is far removed from those deployed in the Great War. Those mines were generally improvised from surplus shells or mortar bombs rather than being purpose-built.

Many buildings and apparently abandoned equipment were referred to as 'mined' (but more properly 'booby-trapped') by retreating German forces using rigged grenades or demolition charges with rather sophisticated fuses. Sometimes those mines exploded after a time delay, occasionally as long as three days, but more often unwary soldiers fell foul of the devices.

Explosives

During the First World War vast quantities of different explosives were used for a multitude of purposes, ranging from the propellants in small-arms cartridges, to the bursting charges of the millions of shells and bombs.

There were further specialized explosives employed by engineers in cutting railway lines or blowing up bridges for their retreating armies. The signal rockets and flares used by the million were a form of explosives. So, too, were the enormous underground mines detonated with such dramatic effect.

Most explosives are substances that undergo violent decomposition accompanied by the formation of large quantities of heat-expanded gas and sudden high pressures. For military purposes, an explosive must be capable of retaining its original stable form until it is required to be detonated – an explosive is by its very nature unstable. The degree of instability has to be precise otherwise it would either be a danger to transport and use or would fail to 'go off' when required.

The many explosives available either detonate or burn at varying rates and each has specific physical characteristics and purpose. Gunpowder, an old general-purpose 'low' explosive, will decompose or burn at around 1,200ft/sec (365m/sec.); whereas for example, TNT, a 'high' explosive will similarly 'decompose' (detonate) at 22,800ft/sec (6,850m/sec) or, to put it another way, at over 4¼ miles per second. Just a slight difference!

For mining purposes the requirement is for an explosive with great lifting potential rather than one that gives a sudden shattering effect. This is achieved by employing a substance with a lower velocity of detonation, rather than a high-speed blast. The aim is to push the material out to create a large crater and not just blast a small hole through it. Indeed some underground mines never broke through to the surface at all. They resulted in an underground cavity, which is called a camouflet. These were often used to destroy the opposition's mining activities using relatively small charges.

Probably the best explosive of all for lifting great masses of earth in mining is gunpowder. It was used initially but its drawbacks over more modern explosives rendered it impractical. It is bulky, very flammable and requires to be tamped (packed in with clay, etc.) for maximum effect. Far more practical is ammonal, which does not suffer the same drawbacks but, being very hygroscopic, must be sealed from damp. As ammonal is several times more powerful than gunpowder (but not too powerful), a considerably smaller mine chamber is required, thereby reducing the attendant risks of digging and shoring a large orifice for the installation of the charge.

Further details on the precise composition of explosives or the methods of initiating an explosion are not appropriate for this book.

Chemical Weapons – Gas

There were many types of gas used in the Great War. Some, such as chlorine, phosgene and mustard were potentially, if not immediately, lethal. Others such as types of teargas were designed to incapacitate rather than kill.

The first known use of chemical weapons in the Great War, in any form, was on 27 October 1914, when 3,000 shells containing *Niespulver* (a form of sneezing agent) mixed with shrapnel, were fired at British and Indian troops. No one seemed to notice the irritant and its use was only discovered after the Armistice. Other inconsequential uses of gas followed but the first significant deployment was by the Germans on 22 April 1915 when clouds of chlorine gas were released from thousands of cylinders dug in near Langemarck and blown by the wind towards St Julien in the Ypres Salient. The British retaliated in kind at Loos in September 1915, but with limited success, as the chlorine gas released from their cylinders drifted back when the wind changed, onto British soldiers.

Most belligerents soon adopted the use of gas and many different types were produced with varying results. The first lethal gas, chlorine, was not particularly efficient once the initial element of surprise was overcome. It was visible, had a strong smell and even simple masks prevented heavy casualties. Phosgene was far more deadly. It was not so easy to detect and often had a delayed action. Perhaps the most unpleasant gas of all was mustard, which was a blistering agent. If inhaled in quantity it slowly destroyed the lungs. If it got on the skin it produced painful burns that were not easy to treat. It was not specifically intended to kill – although it did

Early primitive British gas masks.

produce many fatalities. There were several other gases of varying deadliness tried by both sides.

Gas was initially dispersed from cylinders but soon shells and bombs were developed which could send large quantities of gas into enemy lines regardless of wind direction. One of the most efficient devices was the Livens Projector – a type of mortar that discharged a cylindrical bomb filled with 30lbs of poison gas to a distance of 1,500 yards.

Throughout the summer of 1915 desperate measures were taken to find protection from poison gas. Makeshift pads from cotton waste and even sanitary towels to be soaked by the soldiers in bicarbonate of soda or even urine were sent to the front. Soon the first gas helmets, albeit of limited value, were issued in time for the Battle of Loos. Better protection evolved and eventually the small box respirator, proof against most gases, became standard issue. They were not however the full answer to mustard gas as that could be absorbed through the skin as well as inhaled. They had the additional drawback of limiting a soldier's fighting efficiency because the eyepieces quickly steamed up. Officers in headquarters in the affected zone were not immune. They too had to wear masks as the gases were heavier than air and could penetrate their dugouts.

Warnings of the presence of gas were usually sounded by banging on suspended shell cases that formed quite efficient gongs. A keen eye was also kept on the wind direction, especially in the early days, when gas was dispersed from fixed cylinders.

Although dreaded by soldiers in the war poison gas was not as lethal to British forces as imagined. Russian soldiers are believed to have suffered considerably more from gas poisoning as they were inadequately protected from its effect. British casualties are discussed in Chapter 9.

Miscellaneous Weapons

Flamethrowers

These were mostly portable mechanical devices designed to propel a jet of flammable liquid into the enemy or his positions. The liquid, a thickened form of petrol, was lit, before or after discharge, to burn the victim or set fire to his emplacement. Its first notable use was by the Germans at Hooge on 30 July 1915 but that was not its first outing. The British and French also used flamethrowers but with limited success.

Kukri

This was the weapon of choice of the Gurkha soldier. It is an awesome, exceedingly sharp, curve-bladed knife, used primarily as a chopping rather than stabbing instrument. It is an ideal weapon for fighting in the close confines of a trench, or on a raid to kill sentries or to threaten captured prisoners. The reputation of the much-feared Gurkhas beheading enemy soldiers silently with a kukri, or collecting ears as a count of their tally, always reached their adversaries. They made sure of that. The weapon was used with deadly effect at Neuve Chapelle. No one wanted to meet a Gurkha on a dark night!

Caltrop

This was a rather unpleasant spiked instrument that was scattered by the hundred wherever enemy horses might be present. It was deliberately designed so that no matter which way up it landed, a sharp point would always be uppermost. Its sole purpose was to maim the animal. War is never a pleasant business.

Fléchettes

The First World War fléchette was essentially a mass-produced steel dart, a few inches in length. In the early days of the war, when aircraft began to be used for offensive purposes but aerial bombs were still primitive, quantities of fléchettes were sometimes thrown out of aeroplanes over enemy positions. Both sides used them. Because they were very aerodynamic, by the time they reached earth, they would be travelling at quite a high speed and were quite capable of piercing the body of a soldier on the ground.

Improvised Weapons

Although soldiers were armed at government expense, there were many occasions when the weapons provided did not meet all the requirements of warfare. One such example is close-quarters combat in trenches. The rifle and fitted bayonet were unwieldy items at 5'1" (1.55m) overall length in a trench measuring perhaps three feet wide. The men, on both sides, found that short heavy or sharp items served them better in trench fighting than those provided. It was usual therefore for fighting knives, clubs, etc. to be fashioned from whatever was to hand, and carried into the fray. Whereas France and Germany provided fighting knives in the Great War, the British government did not. Broken bayonets were reshaped and sharpened into very effective weapons by soldiers. Some commercially made knives were available for private purchase. And both sides used their entrenching tools (small spades) to great lethal effect.

Chapter 7

DEATH IN ITS MANY FORMS

The precise medical cause of death was rarely established during the Great War. There was not time, nor was it considered necessary when the obvious overriding cause was by enemy action or, as officially defined, 'battle casualty'. Small statistical samples of wounds of men in hospital were analysed, but the dead were usually classed as 'killed in action' unless certain situations, such as suspected murder, demanded special attention. The medical records of wounded men naturally did show the nature of the injury or disease. Unfortunately virtually all those records were deliberately destroyed a few decades ago. With two-thirds of all British and Dominion fatalities classed as 'killed in action' it is no wonder that our knowledge of how they were killed is incomplete.

For an analysis of those who died see Chapter 10.

Casualty

The term 'casualty' is used in most official publications to include not only those killed but also those wounded, missing or taken prisoner of war. The reason is that, for military purposes, the person, whatever his condition, was not available for battle. To avoid confusion, and where it is not obvious, I have used the terms 'casualty' to include dead and injured, etc., 'fatal casualty' to indicate loss of life and 'wounded' to refer those requiring medical attention.

Categories of Death

In the official casualty lists, *Soldiers (and Officers) Died in the Great War*, there are three main causes of death. They are:

Killed in action	Those who perished as direct result of the war.
Died of wounds	Those who perished as a direct result of war after being first received alive at a medical unit.
Died	Those who died anywhere from non-military causes such as disease or accident.

During the war many men went missing in the heat of battle. Some were captured, some were blown into unidentifiable pieces, some absconded, others simply vanished. Dead bodies were buried as quickly as possible, no matter whether friend or foe. It was simply a matter of hygiene and besides the stench of putrefying flesh was most unpleasant. Such bodies were often unidentified perhaps because the official tags were missing or because there was not time to search properly for one. In consequence that man's identity could never be linked to his resting place. After a period of time – usually one year – the missing man was officially 'presumed dead' if nothing more had been heard. Both sides notified the Swiss Red Cross of prisoners of war as soon as possible but there were lapses in this respect on occasions, perhaps through human error or the inability to identify the prisoner.

The distinction between 'killed in action' and 'died of wounds' does not seem to be officially defined and there is some inconsistency. However, from the detailed examination of many contemporary military documents, it would appear that if a man died from enemy action, or was killed in error by our own forces, *and* before reaching at least the first echelon of organized medical aid, then the category of death was 'killed in action'.

That definition did not take into account how long the man took to die. It could have been immediate or he may have lingered ,for many hours away from medical aid and recording facilities. If a man died having been registered as 'wounded' by the medical authorities then the cause of death would be noted as 'died of wounds'. Men who died from any form of sickness or accident – perhaps in training – were usually recorded as having 'died'. *Soldiers Died in the Great War*, unfortunately, contains many errors and omissions made at the time. It does however show that a staggering 146,443 men died of wounds during the Great War.

Other causes of death are occasionally listed such as 'drowned', 'died (gas poisoning)', 'killed (air raid)' – there are however only a few of these. The Commonwealth War Graves records occasionally give more elaborate details as to the cause of death, especially where a Victoria Cross or Albert Medal has been awarded posthumously. For most of their records, however, there is no indication as to how the serviceman died. A few examples where more information is given about the cause of death are:

Died of diabetic coma contracted in France.
Died of frostbite.
Died of injuries sustained from falling from an aeroplane.
Died of septic poisoning following wounds received in action.
Died of wounds (gas), received at Ypres.
Died of wounds received at the Battle of the Somme 1 July.
Died of wounds while a prisoner of war in a Turkish hospital at Tekrit.
Drowned at sea, while flying off Torquay.
Killed by lightning.
Killed in action at Messines in a gallant attempt to rescue a wounded
  Belgian peasant.
Killed in saving the life of a French boy on the railway lines at Barentin.
Shot by sentence of a German court martial at Bruges.
Shot whilst escaping from German prisoners of war camp.

Compassionately, they do not identify the many tragic instances of suicide committed during the war.

Those deemed to have suffered a 'disgraceful death' – for example by execution – are not usually mentioned in *Soldiers Died in the Great War*. The Commonwealth War Graves Commission records them but the cause of death is not shown. For the differences between these sources of information see Chapter 12.

Instantaneously

Officers and chums of those killed often wrote letters of condolence to the next of kin. Many of these letters survive in national, regimental and private collections. It is amazing how often the word 'instantaneously' occurs, even when it is obvious from the text that the man died some long while after being wounded. Done to console the bereaved that their loved one did not suffer, these letters nevertheless often contain quite graphic accounts of the action and the mortal, but not instantaneously fatal, injuries.

Causes of Death

Friendly Fire

The term 'friendly fire' is only used in this section for index purposes. It is not very friendly to fire on and kill your comrades. The term fratricide (killing one's brother) is also sometimes used. I consider however that, in connection with First World War accidents of this nature, no special phrase is necessary. None appear to have been coined at the time and such incidents were accepted with stoicism. It happened, it was probably unavoidable under the circumstances of the time and it was most unfortunate, but alas accidents will occur during the 'fog of war'.

No one knows how many soldiers on either side were killed or wounded by their friends. It was sufficiently common that separate accounts were not kept. There are a great many official and anecdotal descriptions of incidents where men were accidentally killed by their own side. The numbers of deaths may well run into the tens of thousands during the Great War. The French General Alexandre Percin, a gunnery specialist, estimated that their own artillery accidentally killed around 75,000 Frenchmen.

The causes of death or injury inflicted by one's own side were many but the most common are noted here.

Faulty artillery pieces

The artillery was generally stationed quite a way behind the front-lines and fired over the heads of soldiers into enemy positions. As the war progressed old guns wore out and could not be replaced or totally overhauled in sufficient numbers by the arsenals. After firing a certain number of rounds any artillery piece begins to wear beyond the remedy of field workshops. The gun became considerably less accurate than when it was new, with the result that the shell might fall hundreds of yards short of the intended target onto one's own troops. The 4.7" field gun, originally a naval piece, was notorious for its inaccuracy as it wore out and earned itself the unfortunate nickname 'strict neutrality'. All artillery pieces had the same problem: too much demand and insufficient replacements.

Faulty artillery ammunition

This was equally dangerous and caused a great number of deaths and injury but in different ways. First, if the propellant charge, which fired the shells, was not of sufficient uniformity and quality, those shells would not all arrive at the correct point of aim. They could go over or under. If under, our own soldiers suffered by being hit. If over, the shell would not strike the intended enemy position and in consequence it would not be neutralized. Again our men would suffer. Many shells failed to explode at all and consequently did not do the damage intended to enemy positions or troop concentrations. Sometimes our men were exposed to fire, perhaps as a result of uncut barbed wire that might otherwise have been destroyed. Another situation that caused a great many deaths was the faulty ammunition that prematurely exploded in the barrel of the gun firing it. This was a constant nightmare for the gunners and killed many of them.

Faulty identification of target

This always happens in war. It is tragic but so far no one has found a fail-safe solution. Soldiers are often in a different place to that expected, incorrectly identified as the enemy and fired upon – not only by the artillery but also by the infantry using rifles or machine guns. It is often not possible to positively identify, especially in poor conditions, dirty uniforms that were designed to be inconspicuous. And our lack of up-to-date communications did nothing to relieve the situation.

Calculated risks

In a creeping barrage, shells were exploded ahead of advancing infantry with the intention of killing the enemy and denying access to the ground prior to our infantry taking over. If our soldiers were too far behind the line of moving explosions, any surviving enemy would rise out of dugouts when the barrage had passed over their position and fight our men. To minimize the time the enemy could exploit that situation our men were ordered to keep close to the barrage of shells sweeping ahead of them. If they got too close or if the barrage lacked perfect accuracy some soldiers were killed or wounded. This was accepted as a justified risk at the time.

Similarly, when an underground mine was exploded, it was usual for infantry to rush forward in the race to seize the mine crater – often whilst the debris was still in the air! What goes up will come down. And several hundred tons of rock landing on you is not exactly healthy. Again this was an accepted risk.

Sometimes death came from a very unexpected quarter. There are recorded instances of aircraft, employed observing the fall of shot for the artillery, being hit by a shell from their own side. Captain Cecil Lewis, a fighter pilot with six (plus two shared) victories, wrote a classic account entitled *Sagittarius Rising* in which he describes seeing shells 'hover at [their] peak point' and others whose 'eddies made by their motion flung the machine up and down as if in a gale. Each bump meant that a passing shell had missed the machine by four or five feet.' These shells would have been fired at targets on the ground several miles away. A shell often rose thousands of feet into the air along its trajectory before it commenced its downward plunge. In the case of a 9.2" howitzer that apex could reach 8,000 feet – a typical observation altitude. And a collision is precisely what happened in the example of a Be2a of 2 Squadron Royal Flying Corps. It was brought down by British artillery fire on 10 March 1915 killing the crew. The height here is by no means unique. Many anti-aircraft shells rose to over 28,000 feet. The exceptionally long-range Paris guns, with which the Germans shelled the French capital in 1918 from a range of 115km, sent their shells a staggering 42.3km into the sky on their trajectory. That weapon was in every way incomparable, of course, and employed principles that would not be used again for another fifty years.

Artist's impression of the Paris gun.

Shell-Fire

Artillery was, by a very substantial margin, the greatest cause of death and mutilation during the Great War. Those killed or injured were 'in the wrong place at the wrong time'. The effect on the human body of the blast from explosions capable of destroying heavy masonry, excavating sizeable craters in the earth or ripping apart steel is dramatic. Human bodies often ceased to be recognizable as such.

Shrapnel

One constantly heard the old tale, 'Grand-dad still had lots of shrapnel in him when he died. At one time they used magnets to try and pull it from his body.' This cliché is strictly wrong. True shrapnel consisted of spherical lead balls, as described in Chapter 6, and lead is not attracted by magnets. The effect of being hit by one or more was roughly similar to being hit by rifle or machine gun bullets. Conversely shell splinter, jagged pieces of casing from disintegrating high explosive shells, could come in any shape or size. Some were minute whilst others were large razor-sharp chunks of high velocity steel that could sever a limb, or cause other horrific injuries instantly. And indeed magnets were tried in an attempt to remove them.

Bullet Wounds

The following extract from an account written in December 1914 by Captain Noel Chavasse VC and Bar, RAMC, gives some idea of gunshot wounds.

> The wounds one had to dress were not the clean punctures I had imagined gunshot wounds to be, but because of the near range they at first made one think they had been made by explosive bullets . . . to take an instance of a wound in the fleshy part of the thigh, the entrance wound was neat and punctured, but the exit was a gaping burst, a big hole that I could put my fist into, with broken muscles hanging out. As a matter of fact, I believe that at such near range, the bullet turns over and over, and practically bursts its way out.

As a British doctor, Captain Chavasse was probably examining British soldiers wounded by German bullets. The hydraulic pressures set up by the very high velocity of close-range bullets, inflicting permanent cavitations, most likely caused the traumatic wounds he examined. That applied to military bullets of any nationality. They usually had a heavy core, generally lead, surrounded by a jacket of copper, nickel or steel. However his conclusion may well have been correct if he was examining any wounds caused by British bullets. They were designed with a built-in instability. It was accomplished by filling the front section with aluminium or wood, before the remainder of the jacketed case was filled with lead. This moved the centre of gravity back and caused yawing or tumbling, and hence greater injury, on striking a body.

Conversely, German bullets were solid lead beneath a covering jacket of copper or steel. French bullets, unusually, were not jacketed but made of solid brass. The British practice was not specifically secret but nevertheless not widely advertised. It was perfectly legal, if unconventional, under the various conventions of the time governing war. On the contrary, bullets that were designed to expand upon hitting flesh – so-called 'Dum-Dum' bullets – were banned and anyone caught in possession of them upon capture, by either side, was very harshly dealt with. For practical purposes it makes no difference which bullet hits you, be it from a rifle or machine gun. It was quite likely however that a burst from a machine gun would result in more than one wound.

Bayonet Wounds

The numbers killed in hand-to-hand fighting on either side is unknown. This is because so many statistics were derived by hospitals analysing the types of injuries received by the wounded. The very nature of a fight at extremely close quarters usually involved a duel to the death. Surviving much more than a misplaced flesh wound was unlikely and so relatively few got to hospital to be categorized. Dead bodies were not studied and their cause of death recorded. It must therefore be presumed that far more than the 684 instances recorded in the *Medical History of the War* died from bayonet wounds. It should not however be presumed that vast numbers were killed that way, as most deaths were 'at a distance'.

Snipers

The practice of sniping was not new in 1914. The Germans were exceedingly adept at it and dominated the activity for the first year of the war. Balance was not struck until Major Hesketh-Pritchard, a former big-game hunter, gradually introduced the art and the telescopic-sighted rifles necessary to accomplish it. It was not just the weapon that was important. New skills in long-range shooting and camouflage had to be learnt and practised. A skilful enemy sniper not only causes casualties, he also lowers morale considerably in his area of operations. The slightest exposure would invite a bullet, which invariably struck without warning or the chance to avoid it. Several snipers were credited with well over 100 'kills'. As prime targets themselves, many were in turn sought out and killed by enemy snipers.

Gas

The effects of gas poisoning are always emotive and some of the most dramatic pictures emanating from the war portray soldiers apparently blinded by gas. In reality the number of gas casualties was relatively low. It was not the big killer portrayed by propaganda. The official figures show that 5,899 died from it, which is less than 1 per cent of all fatal casualties. See Chapter 9 for more information.

Daily Attrition and Truces

There were many battles and engagements throughout the war but there were far more days when no formal set-piece battle took place. That does not mean that peace broke out – indeed, far from it. The British policy was one of aggression designed to demoralize the invaders and instil a sense of purpose in our troops. It frequently took the form of trench raids, some of which involved hundreds of soldiers. The latter were not small skirmishes but pitched battles in the area they occurred. They did not happen every day but were nevertheless quite frequent. Even with small-scale raids involving only a few men, it was inevitable that casualties would occur. When there was no actual fighting at all, casualties still mounted up. Trenches were routinely shelled; sniping and random shots were fired. Accidents occurred and disease was always present. There were no days between 5 August 1914 and 11 November 1918 when men in the King's uniform did not die from one cause or other. And that included 25 December 1914 – the day of the Christmas Truce – when forty-one men were reported as killed in action on the Western Front.

The Truce, when large bodies of troops fraternized quite openly on No Man's Land on the Western Front, caused considerable embarrassment to the authorities. To try and ensure it did not happen again, the following uncompromising message from the General Officer Commanding 47 (London) Division was circulated. It was typical of many.

> The GOC directs me to remind you of the unauthorised truce which occurred on Christmas Day in one or two places in the line last year, and to impress upon you that nothing of the kind is to be allowed on the Divisional Front this year.
>
> The Artillery will maintain a slow gunfire on the enemy's trenches commencing at dawn, and every opportunity will as usual be taken to inflict casualties upon any of the enemy exposing themselves.

There were very few transgressions of this order at Christmas 1915 and then it was usually only a short ceasefire for the burial of the dead. Despite this seemingly sensible stance the authorities sought to court-martial those responsible. The British Christmas spirit had drained away.

Live and Let Live

By December 1916 the overall animosity was such that there was no further contemplation of a Christmas Truce. That did not however prevent the situation known as 'live and let live' from occurring on a daily basis throughout the war in some sectors. Very much more subtle than a truce it consisted of, almost invariably, unspoken agreements between the opposing sides. In areas where it occurred, at breakfast time for example, shots were rarely exchanged. This even extended to situations where the local commander, suspecting an informal agreement, ordered fire to be commenced upon the enemy front-line. It has been known for such fire to be aimed high to preserve the status quo. Strangely, considering that the Germans occupied part of France, the French soldiers were especially keen on 'live and let live' agreements. It also occurred in parts of the British front but many units were expressly opposed to it and maintained belligerence at all times.

Accidents and Disease

Many succumbed to illness of one form or other and examples of diseases are discussed in Chapter 9. Altogether over 91,000 officers and men in the army died from non-military causes in the Great War. Accidents and diseases were always present on the battlefields and indeed behind the lines. On average, fifty-eight men died of disease or accident every day.

Death from accidents came in abrupt forms. Many died in training both at home and overseas, from such causes as falling from horses, being run over by wagons and in bayonet exercises. Training large numbers of men in the art of killing, in as short a time as possible, whilst using lethal weapons and live munitions, was fraught with danger. Hand grenades alone resulted in many deaths. Recruits were instructed in the use of live grenades but, until proficient, were a danger to themselves and others. 'Lit' bombs were dropped in the grenade pits rather than thrown down range. Others struck the parapet and rolled back in. In the confined space, carnage resulted from the explosions, and many were killed.

Instructors as well as their trainees were often seriously injured or perished. The Roll of the Albert Medal contains many such instances outlining the courage displayed, as the following example (*London Gazette*, 30457) illustrates:

> The KING has been graciously pleased to award the Decoration of the Albert Medal in recognition of the gallant action of Sergeant Michael Healy, Royal Munster Fusiliers, in saving life in France, in March last, at the cost of his own life. The circumstances are as follows: —
>
> Sergeant Michael Healy, Royal Munster Fusiliers. In France, on the 1st March, 1917, during bombing practice, a live bomb failed to clear the parapet, and rolled back into the trench, which, was occupied by the thrower, an officer, and Sergeant Healy. All three ran for shelter, but Sergeant Healy, fearing that the others would not reach shelter in time, ran back and picked up the bomb, which exploded, and mortally wounded him. Sergeant Healy had previously performed other acts of distinguished gallantry, for which he had been awarded the Distinguished Conduct Medal, the Military Medal, and a bar to the Military Medal. Whitehall, January 1, 1918.

On the same page of that *Gazette* there are three other awards in connection with grenade accidents. And fatal accidents occurred in just about every possible way.

Drowning seems to have been fairly common, with off-duty soldiers jumping blithely into rivers before learning to swim! Others fell into docks, lakes and canals with often fatal results. And that does not include the many poor unfortunates who slipped into mud or deep shell holes on the battlefields and sank from sight before they could be rescued. Not that rescue was often an option in the heat of battle. Most naval deaths were the result of drowning. These of course were not usually accidents but the result of enemy action. Nevertheless a great many sailors were drowned accidentally – often through falling overboard. The ability to swim was not very widespread in 1914.

It was not only on, or on the way to, battlefields that accidents occurred. Early on 19 January 1917 Summertown, London, was rudely awoken by 50 tons of TNT exploding in a purification factory. Around 70,000 properties were damaged and sadly seventy-three people died. Then there was the dreadful accident involving a troop train, a local train and an express on 22 May 1915 at Quintinshill, near Gretna Green, Scotland. Some 214 officers and other ranks died in the crash, plus several civilians.

Executions

Records indicate that, for a variety of offences committed during and shortly after the war, courts-martial pronounced the death penalty on at least 3,118 British, Dominion and Colonial soldiers. And a further 224 death sentences were passed on civilians and prisoners of war for various crimes in areas where military law prevailed. The authority was enshrined in the *Manual of Military Law 1914*, which gave substance to the annually renewable Army Act. Because various records no longer exist, and others are difficult to interpret, it is difficult to be precise about the numbers involved. The figures quoted are the best obtainable.

Although most were sentenced for military offences, other capital crimes such as murder were in evidence. All death sentences had to be individually confirmed by the commander-in-chief of the expeditionary force involved and about 87 per cent were commuted. Altogether 113 Australian soldiers were sentenced to death but none were actually executed, as their government expressly prohibited the death penalty.

A total of 438 executions by the military authorities are believed to have occurred between 4 August 1914 and 31 March 1920. It is calculated that at least 327 of these were of armed service personnel, including three officers, of British, Dominion and Colonial Armies. Others who faced the firing squad were mostly civilians or non-combatants such as coolies or labourers in the Chinese and other Labour Corps. Altogether there were 322 executions in France and Flanders during the war.

Table 6. Figures for Military Executions in the Great War	
Offence	**No. of men executed**
Desertion	266
Sleeping at post	2
Cowardice	18
Disobedience	5
Striking or threatening a senior officer	5
Quitting post	7
Shamefully casting away arms	2
Mutiny	3
Murder	19

At least forty of those shot had been reprieved on earlier occasions for similar crimes and had then gone on to reoffend. One soldier who was shot had been sentenced to death on two previous occasions and each time had his sentences commuted. Recent research shows slight variance on the numbers but the figures in Table 6 are those officially published in 1920 for military executions.

The method of execution was by a firing squad, sometimes comprised of soldiers from the condemned man's own unit. There were usually twelve men in the firing party but this number varied. Sometimes, but not always, one or more rifles was unloaded or reloaded with a blank cartridge, prior to the execution. The firing party were not told which rifles were loaded with live ammunition. (Any experienced soldier would however immediately realize the difference because a blank cartridge has almost no recoil.) On command, a volley was fired into the aiming mark pinned over the heart of the pinioned prisoner. Many shots, intentional or otherwise, missed the intended target. If the man did not die immediately then the officer in charge of the firing party stepped forward and administered the coup de grâce to the head of the condemned man with his pistol.

Morale and Courage

Whatever the cause of death – and a premature and violent demise was highly likely – what was rarely in dispute was the sheer courage and fortitude of the soldiers, sailors and airmen in our armed forces.

An account by Lieutenant Malcolm Kennedy of B Company 2/Scottish Rifles just before the Battle of Neuve Chapelle on 10 March 1915 illustrates this point. An obvious failure by the artillery had resulted in the battalion having to advance against undamaged German defences and barbed wire entanglements. The men were fully aware of the maelstrom of lead and steel that awaited them and that there was a high probability of an unpleasant death.

> The men were in great form, cracking jokes with one another and singing as though they were on a picnic. I went round from time to time to see how they were getting on. Some of them laughingly held out their hands for me to shake, in case either they or I got 'blotted out'. The prospect seemed to amuse rather than upset them, and one realised then, as never before, what a wonderful bunch of fellows

they were, and how damned lucky one was have such men to command. The tragedy of the whole thing is that most of them are now gone. (Papers of Captain M D Kennedy, IWM and Sheffield University)

Their high morale was self-evident and their prophecy was correct, for sadly 162 of them were to be killed within minutes of the battle starting.

Chapter 8

ARMY CORPS

Confusingly, in the army the word 'corps' has two definitions. Here it refers to units, somewhat similar to regiments, whose role was to support the infantry. See Chapter 2 for a definition of 'corps' meaning a subdivision of an army.

The Royal Army Medical Corps (RAMC)

This famous corps had overall responsibility for the general health of the army and the treatment of wounded or sick soldiers. Whether treated at a regimental aid post, field ambulance, casualty clearing station, base hospital or any medical centre, the wounded or sick soldier was the responsibility of the RAMC. They were nobly assisted by the qualified nurses of Queen Alexandra's Imperial Nursing Service. In addition Voluntary Aid Detachments and Red Cross detachments also helped with the sick and injured. See Chapter 9 for further details.

Royal Flying Corps (RFC)

A brief summary is given in Chapter 1.

Royal Regiment of Artillery (RHA, RFA, RGA)

The Royal Regiment of Artillery dates back to 1722 and has a splendid history. In 1899 the regiment split into two groups: the Royal Horse and

Royal Field Artillery in one group and the coastal defence and heavy guns in another, which was named the Royal Garrison Artillery. They did not reamalgamate until 1924.

The First World War was most definitely dominated by the artillery of all belligerents. And, to reiterate, by far the greatest loss of life and greatest number of appalling injuries were caused by artillery fire. The effect of explosions and high velocity jagged pieces of splintered shell on the human body is catastrophic.

Artillery played many roles. The Royal Horse and Field Artillery batteries supported the cavalry and infantry by firing shrapnel at enemy formations and scything down men in the open, attacking – or retreating. Indeed, when the war started, the British only had shrapnel shells for the horse and field artillery guns. The guns used were relatively light and mobile. The Germans did use high explosive shells but they too placed great reliance upon shrapnel. When trench warfare evolved, shrapnel was of no further use for its designed purpose and so the emergence of high explosive and other types of shell resulted. These too were fired by the lighter guns of the Royal Horse or Royal Field Artillery, which were much more manoeuvrable when rapid change of targets was desired. They could not however fire the large shells that were sometimes required.

High explosive shells were fired against various targets within trench systems or against known positions in rear areas. Massive bombardments designed to destroy enemy trench positions and fortifications prior to an attack became the symbol of the artillery. Shells were also used to deny areas of ground to opposing forces and hinder reinforcements. Enemy gun batteries were always a prime objective and most of the 46,605 gunners who died did so in this type of activity. Targets of opportunity, such as vehicles observed moving in the distance, were fired upon. This had the effect of destroying enemy material and also inhibited movement in daylight. Aeroplanes were engaged, with limited success, by specially developed anti-aircraft guns. Likewise tanks were susceptible to artillery fire. In common with all other units, the guns rapidly disappeared from the surface to disguised positions in order to avoid aerial detection and hostile artillery fire. The guns and shells are explained in Chapter 6.

Communication between the front-line infantry and the guns was via the artillery forward observation officers (FOO) and was vital. The infantry needed artillery support and the guns were some distance back. As his title implies, the FOO was the eyes for his guns and, by observing the fall of shot, could direct them onto their objective. He worked alongside the

Artillery forward observation officer with team of Royal Engineer signallers.

infantry in forward and often exposed positions. When telephone contact between him and his battery was lost, the guns could not respond rapidly to any change of target.

Regular and territorial units were similarly armed but the Territorial Force at the beginning of the war often had older guns. The Royal Horse Artillery (RHA) was armed with light guns for the greatest mobility but the 'equipment' (the technical term for a complete gun, carriage and limber) of the Royal Field Artillery (RFA) was also mounted on wheels and transportable. They both fired relatively light shells and had a high rate of fire.

The Royal Garrison Artillery (RGA) was responsible for the big guns. These usually ranged upwards from 6" calibre, were heavy and often not so manoeuvrable. Indeed, many guns were so heavy they had to be dismantled to move them and were often without wheels at all. Some huge guns were mounted on railway carriages.

Guns were laid on their targets. In simple terms that means they were restrained on a stable platform so that the barrels returned to the same position after recoiling from firing each shell. The platform could be purpose-built or just solid ground. Invariably the guns were hidden in pits or elsewhere and direct observation from the gun to target became less frequent as the war progressed. The gun was levelled, precisely aligned on its properly identified target, and increasingly complex indirect fire techniques were used. This is where the skills of the gunnery officers, and the training of the men came into play. With guns commonly shooting from 6,000 to 10,000 and some to over 30,000 yards that skill was paramount.

Bombardments from hundreds of guns firing simultaneously occurred at times during the First World War. For example, in excess of 1¾ million shells of all types were fired by over 1,500 guns during the week preceding and on 1 July 1916, the opening day of the Battle of the Somme. Those figure were well surpassed for the Battle of Messines in June 1917 when, over a similar period of time, 3¼ million shells were fired by more than 2,500 guns. Hundreds of trench mortars added to the maelstrom. Of course most bombardments were not of that intensity but, nevertheless, perhaps as many as one billion shells and mortar bombs were fired altogether on the Western Front during the Great War. The horrendous noise they made permanently ruined the hearing of hundreds of thousands of soldiers and can scarce be imagined by those who did not experience it.

Various terms are used to describe the types of artillery fire used during the war. For example, shrapnel was used to scythe down soldiers caught in the open. Along with high explosive shells, it was also used against aircraft or to cut barbed wire. Counter-battery fire was that specifically targeted against the enemy's artillery emplacements.

Bombardments were munitions aimed at specific enemy positions or areas, such as front-line trenches, defended zones or fortifications, with the purpose of destroying them. Barrages were intended to form an impenetrable barrier – an example being cut-off fire when shells were fired into the area behind enemy positions to prevent reinforcements being rushed forward. Conversely, creeping barrages were fired ahead of advancing formations of soldiers to form a wall of explosions between them and the enemy.

Hurricane fire and drumfire are essentially interchangeable terminology. It was rapid gunfire, at far greater intensities, and usually occurred just before the infantry attacked. Most gunners were quite deaf from the concussion of the guns being fired, despite stuffing cotton waste into their ears.

Various techniques evolved during the war that permitted ever-more-accurate artillery fire without preliminary, ranging shots being fired that betrayed one's intentions. Some such techniques were precise surveying of the ground to improve mapping, accurate interpretation of aerial photographs and meteorological conditions, sound ranging and flash spotting.

Machine Gun Corps (MGC)

The Machine Gun Corps did not come into being until late 1915. Prior to that each infantry battalion was responsible for its own two .303 machine guns – either the Vickers Mk 1 or the older Maxim Machine Gun. In the battalion, a junior officer commanded the machine guns in two sections of six men, each led by a sergeant or corporal. Transport was provided by one cart for the guns and another for the ammunition. By February 1915 the number of machine guns per battalion was increased from two to four when they became available. The use of those guns was however still dictated by the battalion.

Early in 1915 it was decided that the use of machine guns required greater specialization and training than hitherto and an embryonic Machine Gun Corps began to take shape. Specialist training schools were formed and the machine guns were to be withdrawn from battalions to become the responsibility of each brigade. There they formed Machine Gun Companies, each taking as its identity the number of the parent brigade. In order that infantry battalions were not left without any machine guns, those taken away were replaced by light Lewis machine guns – also in .303 calibre – as they became available. This all followed the formation of the Corps on 22 October 1915. A fourth Machine Gun Company, under the control of each division, was desired but could not be completely implemented until April 1917, by which time sufficient guns had became available.

In mid-1918 it was decided further reorganization was necessary. The four machine gun companies within each division were amalgamated into a single machine gun battalion, under the command of a lieutenant-colonel. It took its identity from the parent division. By now the Corps comprised some seventy battalions, each with sixty-four machine guns, and it had a total strength of over 124,000 officers and men. Whereas most of the Corps was with the infantry, other units served with the cavalry. The Motor Machine Gun Branch was mobile, with its guns mounted on sidecars or armoured vehicles. The Heavy Branch went on to become the Tank Corps in July 1917.

Machine guns firing long bursts were deadly to an enemy and became a prime target to be sought out and destroyed. As they were often in static positions they were not too difficult to locate, no matter how well disguised. This resulted in the death of nearly 14,000 of the men from the Machine Gun Corps. From being a comparative rarity in 1914, the number of machine guns available to the British Army on the Western Front rose to 52,358 by November 1918.

Royal Engineers [RE]

The Royal Engineers were arguably the most versatile unit of the army in the Great War. They fulfilled many roles, ranging from infantry, when required, to specialist artisans. The basic rank of a Royal Engineer is a sapper. By definition, a sapper originally specialized in digging saps, that is, tunnels towards enemy positions. A sapper was however trained in many other skills. He was also expected to fight if need be and in consequence was armed accordingly. Such was the demand for their expertise that their numbers grew from around 25,000 in 1914 to well over 300,000 by the Armistice. These figures include the transportation sections. Most sappers belonged to field companies that were distributed throughout the army. Each company consisted of around 220 officers and men at full strength and initially two, soon to be three, such companies was attached to every division. Others were attached to higher echelons of command.

Among their jobs was the design and construction of fortifications, a traditional role for the corps. They were instrumental in building the vast network of trenches on the Western Front. That is not to say they did all the spadework – the infantry did much of the actual digging, but under guidance from the engineers.

They were also responsible for the construction and maintenance of countless miles of road and railway track to bring up vital war supplies. Likewise the canals were in their charge. They were proficient in building bridges, road and railway tunnels and maintaining an efficient water supply for men, horses and machines. Most horses were shod by their farriers. Pigeons too were their responsibility. Engineers repaired almost anything, ranging from weapons to wells, and they made most of the early improvised hand grenades. They were also adept in the art of demolition.

The storage and discharge of poison gas was the responsibility of special companies. Other companies surveyed the land and made maps. A description of all their tasks could fill a book. But perhaps one task for which they were justly famous was tunnelling under enemy lines. After all, they were sappers!

Tunnelling

Early tunnelling was rather haphazard. It started mainly out of necessity to counter enemy mining and employed previous miners taken from the ranks. Formed into brigade mining sections they went underground with whatever materials were available. Major John Norton Griffiths had been a civil engineer with considerable experience of tunnelling for sewers in London and Manchester. He suggested that specialist miners be recruited and sent immediately to France to commence burrowing, or 'moling', beneath the German lines and then explode mines to destroy the enemy defences. After considerable bureaucratic delay the idea was finally approved, but only after several German mines had exploded beneath British trenches.

Miners were hastily 'volunteered', convinced by a prospective huge pay rise, given uniforms and sent directly to France. The backbone of the new force were 'clay-kickers'. They employed a technique using specially adapted spades and a wooden frame to lie on underground. This enabled spits of clay to be cut from the tunnel face with minimum effort where there was insufficient room to use traditional picks and shovels. At the end of each tunnel a chamber was excavated and packed with explosives. The tunnel was sealed and the mine exploded when required.

The new force rapidly grew in strength and successful operations commenced from mid-1915. The burrows they dug turned the Western Front into a two-tier system with moles eventually creating a subterranean world beneath much of the front. Mines were exploded regularly, which caused trepidation among soldiers not knowing if they were going to be

Clay-kicker with grafting tool and cross.

The famous explosion of the Hawthorne Ridge Redoubt Mine which, at 07.20 on 1 July 1916, signalled the start of the Battle of the Somme.

blown sky high without warning. They could sometimes avoid approaching shells or mortar bombs – they could not avoid a mine. Hundreds of mines were exploded in France and Belgium but surely the most famous was at Beaumont Hamel. Anticipated to be 65ft beneath a German redoubt, 40,600lbs (18,500kg) of explosives were detonated at 07.20 on 1 July 1916. This finally launched the Battle of the Somme. It was filmed erupting by Geoffrey Malins and this has frequently been shown on television. Another huge crater at La Boisselle is still evidence of the destructive power of a mine. The debris from that explosion rose over 4,000ft into the air. The most ambitious undertaking must surely be the mining in advance of the Battle of Messines. With galleries up to 2,160ft (980m) in length, at least twenty-two mines were excavated. Eventually, on 7 June 1917, nineteen of them, packed with almost one million pounds of explosives, erupted beneath the German lines and enabled a breakthrough in that sector.

Listening posts utilizing sensitive geophones, devices for amplifying underground movement, were established to try and detect enemy mining activities. Each side regularly attempted to disrupt the opposition's tunnelling achievements by counter-mining and exploding small charges underground to collapse their workings. It was not unknown for the two sides to meet as a result of merging tunnels and then fierce fighting in the darkness often ensued. Mine rescue stations containing primitive breathing apparatus were established to attempt the rescue of men trapped or overcome by fumes underground.

Communication

The Signal Service was formed in 1908 as a separate branch of the Royal Engineers and signal companies were attached to most army formations. They were responsible for maintaining the system from the various headquarters to the front-lines. Despite many heroic deeds repairing broken wires, they and infantry soldiers assisting them were fighting an uphill struggle. Around 2,000 men in the Signal Service alone, plus many hundreds of signallers in the infantry, were to die during the Great War.

Communication, or rather lack of it, was arguably the biggest problem of the First World War. It was mostly by telephonic means, connected by a network of very vulnerable cables, run along trenches or buried in the ground. These cables enabled conversation between front and rear areas. In an offensive operation, cables could rarely be laid quickly enough to keep pace with the advance. And none could be laid to connect units on either side that were also moving forward. There was no effective way, therefore, for two advancing battalions to speak to each other.

Alternative methods of conveying messages were of limited value. Visual signalling was not usually practical. Pigeons could take messages but naturally not return with any reply! Dogs were used occasionally. Radio transmitting and receiving equipment was bulky and heavy and required large accumulators for power. It was not available to forward troops for most of the war. The early aerials were large, probably exposed and vulnerable. Signals were easily intercepted by direction-finding equipment, with potentially dire consequences. In addition, such radios as existed were relatively short-range and few in number. Some had notable success but most wireless communication available was retained for use between higher echelons of command at rear bases. It was used at times to send signals in Morse code from aircraft to the ground to indicate targets, the primitive transmitters being powered from the aircraft's generator. Semi-portable sets, which could utilize much smaller aerials, became available in limited numbers from late 1917 but were not widely used.

Where telephones were impossible or failed, by far the most commonly employed alternative was the human message carrier or 'runner'. It was a most dangerous job. A man, probably an infantryman, would be despatched to go to another unit or higher command with a written message. He, or another, then had to retraverse the broken battlefield, often under fire, with the response. If the runner(s) survived, the time taken between request and reply could be several hours. And by that time the question, in the heat of battle, may no longer have been relevant.

Tank Corps

Code-named a 'tank', to disguise its true purpose, the weapon along with its corps slowly lurched into being. Conceived by Lieutenant-Colonel Ernest Swinton as early as 1914, it took the intercession of Winston Churchill to get the beast into service. It first saw action at the Battle of Flers-Courcelette on 15 September 1916 under the command of the Heavy Branch of the Machine Corps. In that action thirty-two Mark 1 tanks, each weighing 28 tons, were deployed. They were mechanically unreliable and unfortunately fourteen either broke down or became ditched. There were two variations of heavy tank, each having a crew of eight. The male was

Tanks excelled at crushing barbed wire entanglements.

armed with two 6-pounder guns, one in the purpose-built sponson attached to each side. The female version was equipped with five Vickers machine guns. Their top speed was less than four miles per hour. Many models succeeded the Mark 1 but were all somewhat similar in appearance and firepower. Lighter and much faster tanks, such as the Whippet, were introduced in early 1918. The Tank Corps itself was formed on 27 July 1917.

Notable successes for tanks were at the Battle of Cambrai in November 1917, at Amiens in August 1918 and in the final advance. In those actions tanks were deployed in their hundreds, better tactics had been evolved and they were more mechanically reliable. Some had wireless sets and could receive messages but were not able to transmit from within the hull. No wireless inter-tank communication was possible during the war. Sadly, all First World War tanks were relatively lightly armoured and vulnerable to even light artillery fire. Perhaps one of their best uses was in crushing and dragging away barbed wire entanglements to enable the infantry to advance.

Army Service Corps (ASC)

Unless fighting soldiers are continually resupplied with materials of war no battles could ever be won. And the organization that supplied it was the Army Service Corps. They not only carried the materials of war – which could be anything from bullets to biscuits – they also frequently processed that material. For example, the flour that they carried was frequently baked into bread by Army Service Corps bakers.

Fielding only a tiny force in 1914, the Corps grew to number to over 325,000 men. Their role changed to suit requirements and many men were transferred to infantry battalions to fight when required. The rather unkind nickname of 'Ally Sloper's Cavalry' does not take into account the fact that around 8,500 officers and men died of various causes with the corps. It is not well-known, for example, that in the first tank action at Flers-Courcelette most of the drivers were members of the Army Service Corps. The drivers of ambulances, both horse and mechanical, were ASC men.

The subunit of the Army Service Corps was the company and there were over 1,200 companies. Most were numbered (e.g. 136 or 1082), but some had names such as Auxiliary Water Company or No. 3 Donkey Company. They had many specific roles and were allocated throughout all the armies as required. Many formed part of the divisional train that supplied goods to fighting units. Others were higher up the resupply chain, moving material from England to base depots, railheads, etc. Stores were maintained throughout the war zones. Remount companies and squadrons were involved in breaking and training horses ready for the army. The jobs of the ASC are too numerous to be listed here. One group does however deserve special mention. The Wolds Wagonars (sic) were a group of qualified civilian wagon drivers formed into a special reserve in 1912. Volunteers from the Yorkshire Wolds were enrolled with a small retainer and in 1914, when their services were required, were mobilized and were sent with virtually no military training to France, where they served with distinction. It was their skill at driving the heavy general service (GS) wagons that was required, not their saluting abilities.

In 1914 most stores were moved by horse-drawn transport and overall the animals required a total of over 2,500,000 tons of hay and 3,250,000 tons of oats to keep them provisioned during the war. Horses were widely used, not just for transport. The Royal Horse and Field Artillery guns were horse-drawn and officers and many men were mounted. Horses, mules or donkeys pulled many items of equipment, such as general service wagons and ammunition carts. Lots of shells were carried into action by pack animals where it was impossible for vehicles to travel. Hundreds of thousands of horses were purchased from overseas and the army in Britain commandeered many others. Sadly, at the end of the war, relatively few of

Army Service Corps 3-ton lorry (American Pierce Arrow).

those seized were returned to their former owners. Most remained abroad. Of the 828,360 transport animals supplied, it is thought around 500,000 horses and 250,000 mules perished as a result of the war; many were sold for meat when it was over.

The Army Service Corps was certainly not slow to accept mechanical transport and its first vehicles arrived in 1903. By August 1914 there were 507 vehicles already in service, ranging from cars and lorries to ambulances and steam tractors. Vehicles purchased and requisitioned on mobilization increased this figure to well over 1,300. By the Armistice that number had risen to about 120,000 vehicles of all descriptions and more and more items, formerly transported by horse, were hauled by lorries. The Army Service Corps supplied the lifeblood of the Army, with men working continuously and mostly thanklessly in their tasks. I have never ceased to be amazed, for example, how drivers were able to locate, at night and with no lights on their vehicles, isolated gun batteries to resupply them with shells.

In recognition of the vital role played by the Army Service Corps during the war it was granted the title of 'Royal' on 27 November 1918.

Labour Corps and Similar Units

Given the nature of the Western Front, accommodation had to be constructed, fortifications built, and thousands of miles of trenches dug. Lines of communication in the shape of roads, railways and canals had to be built and maintained. Ships had to be loaded and unloaded – likewise trains, supply dumps and distribution points. This all took up huge amounts of manpower – manpower the Army could ill afford to take from the combat forces. And yet somehow those vital jobs had to be done. Army Service Corps and Royal Engineer soldiers performed many of the skilled jobs but there was still a vast amount of semi-unskilled work to do – much of it digging or carrying. The partial answer was to recruit labourers from wherever they could be found.

Initially labourers sent from Britain were grouped into Labour Companies of the Army Service Corps and the Labour Battalions of the Royal Engineers. Most were eventually absorbed into the Labour Corps when it was created in February 1917.

With the chronic shortage of labour, desperate measures were taken. Men were brought in from all parts of the Empire and places such as China and Egypt to help. Pioneer Battalions were created from ordinary infantry battalions – often from the Territorial Force, where their mix of civilian trade skills was invaluable. They were trained soldiers but normally engaged on labouring or construction work unless called upon to fight.

The Labour Corps grew to huge proportions and eventually numbered in excess of 389,000. On occasions of crisis men from the Labour Corps were armed and fought as infantry. Of over 5,000 men from the Corps who died in the war, 2,309 are recorded as being killed in action or dying from wounds.

Other sources of labour came from infantry labour battalions composed of men medically graded as unsuitable to fight. Conscientious objectors were formed into Non-Combatant Companies. Even enemy prisoners of war were put to work. And women contributed to the war effort. The Women's Auxiliary Army Corps was formed in March 1917, later to become the Queen Mary's Army Auxiliary Corps. They were engaged in basic tasks that officially did not require too much heavy labour. That said, having seen pictures of women working with large munitions, I rather suspect they took their fair share of hard work along with their men-folk.

Royal Defence Corps (RDC)

This corps consisted of mostly older men and others unfit for front-line duties. Many were already serving in various home service garrison battalions and were, from August 1917, amalgamated with others in reserve battalions. Their duties, none of which were overseas, were guarding various establishments and prisoners of war and helping with anti-aircraft observation.

Other Corps

There were several other corps whose names, listed below, largely indicates the responsibilities they undertook. Each was essential and played a vital role in the overall smooth running of the army and the conduct of the war. Unfortunately space does not permit further amplification here.

Corps of Military Police
Military Provost Staff Corps
Intelligence Corps
Army Veterinary Corps
Army Ordnance Corps
Army Pay Corps
Army Chaplain's Department

Chapter 9

MEDICAL MATTERS

The Royal Army Medical Corps (RAMC) had overall charge of the general health of the army and the treatment of wounded or sick soldiers. Whether treated at a regimental aid post, field ambulance, casualty clearing station, base hospital or any medical centre, the wounded or sick soldier was the responsibility of the RAMC. Stretcher-bearers were often taken from infantry units and attached to, rather than transferred to, the RAMC.

Wounds

The causes of wounds are often the same as those where the injury resulted in death. Not all wounds were initially life-threatening but could prove to be so if not treated promptly and properly. Despite the lack of certain techniques we presently take for granted, the medical services were highly efficient where the patient could be treated in time. And they continued to improve greatly as the war progressed. In war conditions it was unfortunately simply not possible to rescue injured men speedily. Operational matters often took priority over the evacuation of the wounded. Men and transport required for fighting could not be spared to help.

When we consider the type of wounds soldiers received in the Great War, we also have to consider the possible treatments available at the time. And what was not yet available.

Wounds to the body, however caused, result in blood loss. The loss of large quantities of blood, which is not rapidly replaced, will result in death. Blood transfusion was not properly developed during the war. Prior to 1910

The popular concept of the wounded soldier. Sadly the reality was often horrendously different.

any transfusions had to be direct between donor and recipient, because of the problems of coagulation. The science of refrigeration and storage of blood was in its infancy and blood type incompatibility was not fully understood. Transfusions would not have been possible on the battlefield – the one place where they would have had the most dramatic effect – to save lives after traumatic injuries. Any transfusions at base hospitals, rare before 1917, would have been risky. In short, a great number of wounded soldiers, sailors and airmen simply bled to death on the battlefields from often relatively simple wounds. A tourniquet is a mechanical device to totally block the flow of arterial blood by means of compression. If available, they were used to staunch the flow of blood, but they were no use if too much had already flooded away. Nor was the detrimental effect of keeping a tourniquet on too long fully appreciated. The treatment of many conditions prescribed by Royal Army Medical Corps wartime training manuals often differs radically from twenty-first-century medical practice.

Another great saviour of human life – antibiotics – would not become available until the Second World War. It was, and still is, rare for any penetrating injury caused by a foreign body such as a bullet, shell fragment or bayonet to be clean. The foreign body would usually carry particles of dirty uniform or other matter into the wound and an infection would result and spread. Infections often developed into septicaemia or, even worse, gas gangrene, which had its origins in the soil. The management of these complications would have been much easier if antibiotics had been available. As it was, the only treatment was prevention by the use of antiseptics. Many were employed; indeed within the larger wound dressings was an ampoule of iodine. Sphagnum moss dressings, impregnated with garlic, were also tried, as they had antibacterial and water (body fluid) absorbing qualities.

Others in use included carbolic acid, boric acid, potassium permanganate and many mercury compounds that often had rather nasty side effects. Once a major infection had set in, amputation of the offending limb was often the only course of action possible. If the infection was to a wound in the trunk of the body, death was highly likely.

X-ray examination, anaesthesia and morphine-based drugs for pain relief were available during the war. Surgical techniques, to remove bullets, shell fragments and to repair injuries, improved throughout the war as more and more patients were operated upon. Just as important was the dedication and care of most surgeons, doctors and nurses. Following surgery to remove foreign bodies, clean and drain wounds, repair or amputate shattered limbs, etc., much depended upon the nursing care available. Over 41,000 men had limbs amputated and sadly, on average, 10 per cent died. This number rose to 28 per cent if gangrene set in. Despite the difficulties, by far the greatest number of wounded men returned to duty after treatment.

Plastic surgery, although experimented with in earlier years, was not normally available. However between 1920 and 1925 some 2,944 facial repair operations were performed at Queen Mary's Hospital, Sidcup. More usually, facial masks were cast and painted, to cover the worst disfigurements. Artificial limbs

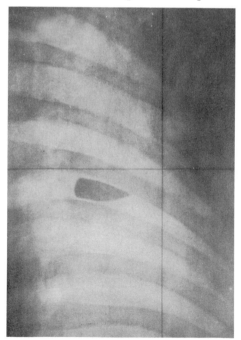

1915 X-ray showing a bullet lodged in the right lung of a soldier.

were produced and supplied to those who had lost limbs but they were primitive by today's standards of prostheses.

Initial Treatment

Unless able to walk to get help, many wounded soldiers had to treat themselves initially until a stretcher-bearer could reach them. It was forbidden for a soldier advancing into battle to stop and assist a wounded comrade. In basic training the subject of first aid was not given much prominence and so common sense had to take over. Inside each soldier's tunic was sewn a first field dressing. This was a sterile bandage with a gauze pad attached. This basic item of kit was often all that was available. Assuming rescue from the field of battle, the man would be assisted perhaps on a stretcher, to the nearest 'regimental aid post' (RAP), sometimes called the 'battalion aid post'. That would consist of an improvised shelter close to the fighting zone. It was generally staffed by a medical officer (doctor) and several men of the Royal Army Medical Corps, plus others allocated by battalions to act as stretcher-bearers and carry out other basic tasks. The job of the doctor was to stabilize the wounded man to try and prevent him from dying before the next stage of treatment. There was neither time nor facilities to do much more than bandage up wounds, administer morphine and record the dosage on the patient. The wounded soldier then commenced a journey via several establishments, each of which performed vital medical and filtering processes. The number of stretcher-bearers available increased as the war progressed.

Evacuation

Field Ambulance

The next stage was to a 'field ambulance' that served many functions. Elements of it were often located miles apart. Doctors and medical orderlies staffed the various elements. Often the journey there would be hazardous and difficult for the stretcher-bearers trying to negotiate narrow, muddy, trenches and even narrower traverses whilst carrying a heavy human burden. They were the first place a man might realistically expect more than cursory treatment. Field ambulances were not off-road vehicles equipped with sirens and flashing lights!

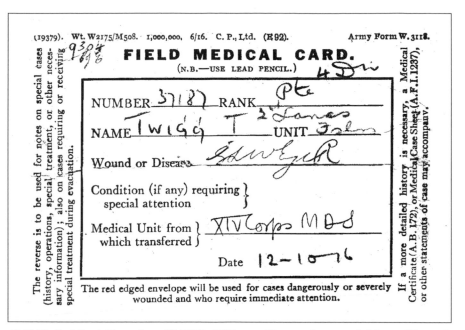

Field Medical Card (Army form W. 3118). NB 'gsweyeR' = gunshot wound right eye. The cards were enclosed in a waxed envelope and attached to the patient.

One aspect of their duties was to establish an advanced dressing station (ADS) close to the front. It would serve perhaps four regimental aid posts. On arrival, bandages and splints could be checked, the patient given drinks, if appropriate, and made a little more comfortable. And forms were filled in. The Field Medical Card, completed for casualties, recorded the progress in treatment. It is interesting to note that in June 1917 the War Office ordered a new batch of 1,750,000 such cards. The war was far from over!

The casualty was then despatched, perhaps by horse or motor ambulance, to the next echelon – the main dressing station of the field ambulance. Here his condition was reviewed. In the case of relatively minor injuries, the soldier would be patched up and, after a period of rest, returned to his battalion to continue his duties. If he had more serious injuries they would be examined, cleaned and treated. Sometimes this involved life-saving surgery at a nearby advanced operating station.

Each division had three field ambulances attached to it. Field ambulances had many other responsibilities but the main one relevant here was to be responsible for transportation of the casualty between its various units.

Casualty Clearing Station (CCS)

Motor ambulance convoys, sometimes assisted by the field ambulance, would then take the man to the next link in the medical chain – the 'casualty clearing station'. A casualty clearing station was generally a large, fully equipped, often tented hospital set up around ten miles behind the front. It rarely kept patients for more than a few days. Their primary job was collection of casualties from allocated field ambulances, to tackle more complex conditions and prepare the patient for dispersal to the next level. They were able to X-ray and perform major operations on a lot of men, under far more favourable conditions than those at a field ambulance. Often, after a battle, a great many casualties required expert medical attention simultaneously. The CCS was better equipped and staffed to deal with that situation, although inevitably delays in receiving aid occurred. In addition to surgery they gave much needed comfort and stabilized the patient ready for his onward journey. The patient could be returned to his unit if sufficiently recovered. Or he could be placed upon an ambulance train, hospital barge or other conveyance and taken onwards.

Any echelon could be by-passed if circumstances warranted it. Thus, for example, casualties deemed by the doctors to have no realistic chance of survival were retained at the place they were so assessed and placed in the local moribund tent or ward. There they would be given every possible comfort, nursing care and painkillers, but effectively left to die. Unfortunately patients with severe abdominal or head wounds were often untreatable, given the conditions at the time. Over 43 per cent of those wounded in the abdomen subsequently died. With the huge numbers of more lightly

Field Service Post Card that broke the rules! Pte B Burrows was subsequently killed in action, 23 Aug. 1918.

wounded men flooding in who stood a greater likelihood of survival, available resources were allocated to them in preference to those most likely to die anyway. It was harsh, but it was during a war nearly a century ago.

Further treatment and long-term care would be undertaken at huge, fully equipped general, stationary or base hospitals often located near the large costal towns such as Boulogne, Calais and Etaples. These hospitals specialized in certain injuries and in consequence the patient would, hopefully, be sent to the appropriate one for his condition. The main remaining type of hospital was the home hospital. And to be sent there was the wounded soldier's greatest desire – back home to Blighty! (Blighty derives from the old army in India where *belati* was Hindi for 'far away' (home).) Field Service Post Cards were provided for the wounded but strict rules applied. Note the patient could only say how well he was! Sadly death sometimes preceded that letter 'to follow at first opportunity'.

Ailments

Service personnel are no different from civilians when it comes to catching a cold or flu or any other ailment prevalent among the human race. What was different was the treatment. Many poorer people at the time of the Great War never or rarely saw a doctor, as he had to be paid. There was no National Health Service. Illnesses were often left to run their course. The patient recovered or the patient died – and all without medical intervention. The better off could afford medical attention but there was, in reality, not that much that was beneficial for bacterial or viral infections.

In the armed forces medical aid was available free and doctors were on hand to prescribe appropriate treatment. What was lacking was the equivalent of 'bedside manner'. Men had to parade to see the doctor who, from many accounts, rarely had much sympathy with the presumed malingerer who stood in front of him. After all, the serviceman, on attestation, had once been certified as fit for military service. Commonly, the prescribed remedy was M & D – that is, medicine and (return to) duties. More often that not the medicine prescribed was a 'Number 9' pill. Laxatives were the favourite antidote for most illnesses at the time. I know of one instance where the patient, seriously ill with Spanish Flu in 1918 was prescribed castor oil. He was not best pleased but eventually recovered to tell the tale. Perhaps castor oil was all that the overworked doctor had. Even today there is no cure for the common cold or the flu virus.

The Army was well aware from previous campaigns that certain diseases killed more men than bullets. Those diseases were typhoid, dysentery, cholera and diarrhoea. Officers were trained to pay particularly attention to hygiene, as prevention was always better than cure. Because of this care, deaths from those diseases were comparatively rare on the Western Front.

Life in the trenches or behind the lines was not particularly healthy and often the strength of a unit was deficient through sickness. It is impossible to cover them all but a few notes may illustrate the typical health problems that prevailed. Soldiers suffered from, and a ratio died from, just about every disease known. The incidence obviously depended to a great extent upon the theatre of war he was assigned to.

Dentistry

Dental hygiene was not uppermost in the minds of either servicemen or the army council, despite the official issue of toothbrushes. With more and more sugar in the diet, dental decay and toothache was common. And the easiest treatment was extraction of the offending tooth. The local anaesthetic Novocain was in existence but rarely used in war zones. Although teeth were being filled by the time of the Great War, the dentists' drill was foot operated, bulky and only available overseas in base hospitals. The manufacture of false teeth was however well established and no longer relied upon 'Waterloo Teeth' – which were those formerly gathered from dead soldiers after a battle. The actual teeth were totally false, made of porcelain and were set in vulcanite. Many officers had high-quality false teeth made and fitted whilst on leave. For others, the Army Dental Service made tens of thousands of new dentures to aid the toothless. Extractions always exceeded repairs and fillings.

Drunkenness

Alcohol and its consumption in excess was a condition well-known to the Army and did not pose any real problem. The possible long-term degeneration of the men's livers was not their concern. Minor punishments for drunkenness were liberally handed out to offenders who, when sober again, continued their tasks as if nothing had happened. Hangovers were not accepted as an excuse for sick leave.

Dysentery

Dysentery was another great cause of losses to the Army. Insanitary conditions, common in warfare, were the prime cause – a factor well recognized by the authorities who fought hard to control it. Contact with faeces, whether alone, in soiled ground, in enemy positions or combined with rotting bodies, was the chief culprit. Once an area is contaminated it is very difficult under war conditions to clean it. Personal hygiene was generally not possible in the trenches. Of all the signs I have seen in museums, and in photographs associated with trench life, the one I have never noticed is 'and now wash your hands'. Thirsty men crave water to such a degree that even obviously polluted water is better than no water. The sanitary arrangements improved as the war progressed, with great emphasis being placed on latrines and the proper disposal of their contents. Nevertheless some 203,421 men were admitted to hospital during the war with dysentery and hundreds died of it.

Gas Poisoning

Gas was a much-feared weapon of war but the number of related casualties was relatively low. It is estimated about 186,000 British soldiers suffered from gas poisoning. By far the majority recovered – at least in the short term, but more than 5,899 are officially known to have died. That figure does not include many Canadian soldiers who were in the forefront of the first poison gas attack on the Western Front on 22 April 1915. It could also be an underestimate as many men were simply recorded as 'killed in action' in the pandemonium that day. However, as most poison gases used in the Great War were not immediately lethal, the numbers are unlikely to be much higher. The majority of victims reached medical aid and were then accurately categorized as gas casualties. Rather less than 10 per cent of all admissions were the result of gas.

Of those who seemed to recover, many were to die young from the detrimental effects of poisonous gas on their lungs. The number of these is totally unknown, as they would have already been discharged from the Army. Those premature deaths would no doubt have contributed significantly to the total number of war-related deaths, had records been kept.

All forms of gas, whether potentially lethal or not, were primarily intended to create fear and confusion and then incapacitate and demoralize the victims. An injured soldier with a difficult incapacity requires far more manpower, equipment, expertise and expense than one who is killed outright.

Influenza

Flu, along with the common cold, was quite common during the Great War and not normally life-threatening. Here though, we are briefly considering the much more deadly virus that was popularly called 'Spanish Flu'. The name seems to have originated after widespread reporting of many cases in the uncensored Spanish press. Scientists still debate its exact origins and the precise type of flu strain involved, neither of which is relevant here. The flu seems to have come in several waves, starting in March 1918, with the main pandemic gathering pace from August that year. The disease continued into 1919 but finally came to an end almost as abruptly as it started, leaving whole communities devastated. Both sides in the war were equally affected. Various sources suggest it originated in the United States, but again there are many contenders for this dubious honour. The numbers of people worldwide who caught the flu is unknown but estimates of 50 to 100 million deaths from it are probably accurate. Strangely, it seems to have been deadliest to the young, fit and healthy members of the community rather than the old, weak and malnourished. Robust American soldiers suffered rather badly – indeed proportionally worse than seasoned troops from Britain, who had already endured several years of trench privations. It was a most virulent outbreak and often resulted in massive haemorrhaging in the lungs resulting in the victims literally drowning in their own blood.

Malaria

Almost half a million British troops were treated for malaria during the Great War and about 3,000 died from it. Incidence was highest in Macedonia, East Africa, Mesopotamia, Egypt and Palestine. But there were also some 9,022 cases in France and Flanders – with at least fourteen resultant deaths. To give some idea of the severity of the disease, in Macedonia battle casualties totalled 23,762; that is men no longer able to fight because they were dead, wounded, missing or prisoners of war. In the same theatre of war 162,517 men were incapacitated by malaria. The only effective treatment for malaria was quinine, which can cause undesirable side effects.

Self-Inflicted Injuries

From their very nature this condition was disguised from the medical authorities and attributed by the injured man as either caused by enemy action or an accident. The penalties for deliberately wounding oneself were very severe. As the culprit obviously planned to survive the incident, the relatively minor injury was almost invariably to an extremity such as a hand or foot. Occasionally the fleshy parts of an arm or leg might be injured but at risk of serious long-term damage. Indian soldiers in France were under the unfortunate illusion that if they were wounded in action in any way they would be sent home to India to recover. Some did not want to be in France at all but others genuinely believed that an injury was most honourable and that, as a result, they had entirely fulfilled their duty. In consequence of this false belief it became a practice to try to sustain a minor injury. Several instances are recorded of men, not only Indian soldiers, raising a hand above the parapet as an invitation to German sharpshooters who naturally were happy to oblige. A shot-off finger seemed a small price to pay to get out of the war. Because of this, instances of hand wounds where no other injuries were present were viewed with great suspicion. Sometimes drugs or chemicals were consumed to fake serious illness, but again the medical authorities were generally well aware of this and retained the man, under close observation, to await natural recovery. In practice, especially early in the war, only severely wounded men from India were repatriated back home. The total number of instances is obviously unknown but 3,904 officers and men were convicted of self-inflicting a wound to escape military service.

Shell-Shock

This is the common name given to the condition of patients suffering from nervous disorders or mental illnesses caused by the stress of war. It was officially, if recognized at all, called neurasthenia during the Great War. Sometimes men, obviously incapable of reason, were classified as 'not yet diagnosed (neurological)'. Others were simply said to be suffering from 'lack of moral fibre'. If the man ran away in his distressed condition, he might well, upon capture, be charged by the military authorities with desertion. The term 'post-traumatic stress disorder' would not be applied until 1980. Shell-shock, in whatever guise, was simply not generally understood, or accepted, as a reason not to fight. Treatment was mostly primitive or even brutal in spartan mental institutions unless the patient was lucky enough to be sent to one of the few specialist hospitals such as Craiglockhart War Hospital. There, a psychiatrist, William H Rivers, used several clever and revolutionary techniques to help cure those in his charge. Hypnotism, drugs and electric shocks were used, along with much kindness and understanding. For example, he reversed the old practice of banning the patient from actively thinking of the grisly situations that had caused the breakdown – only for the deranged soldier to have vivid and uncontrollable nightmares on sleeping. Instead, Rivers encouraged the man to modify the memories to either get some solace or perhaps black humour from what had happened. His treatment helped many. Among his famous patients were Siegfried Sassoon and Wilfred Owen. Unfortunately few records were kept of the condition and so we do not know how many cases were involved. It did however run into several tens of thousands.

Trench Foot

Sometimes called immersion foot and loosely linked with frostbite, this debilitating condition was especially bad during the first part of the war. The British Expeditionary Force had moved to the Ypres Salient, which has a very high water table. The trenches were invariable wet, and more often than not flooded. Men were obliged to stand for long periods in cold water with inadequate protection. The standard army boots did not keep out water that was deeper than the boot and even shallower water soon seeped through the leather. Indeed, the boots may well have been restrictive and, together with tightly wrapped puttees, exacerbated the problem. (Puttees are long strips of wool serge wound spirally around the lower leg, over the top of the boot, to below the knee. They were intended to offer protection and support as well as keeping dirt and small creatures from entering the boot. The origin of the name is the Hindi *patti* (bandage). The illustration of a British Tommy 4/Middlesex 1914 shows them being worn.) Trench foot, unlike frostbite, does not require freezing temperatures and can break out after as little as half a day's exposure. Initially the feet go numb and then turn blue or red and blister. Unfortunately the soldier would probably have had more pressing matters to deal with during the fighting around Ypres than to examine the colour of his insensitive feet. By the winter of 1915/16 the authorities realized the gravity of the situation and introduced preventative measures. These included the use of duckboards, sumps and pumps to ease the water problem. Additionally there was frequent inspection of the men's feet, whale oil was liberally applied to them and socks were regularly changed. Gradually trench waders were provided for the wettest areas. Unfortunately, before the condition was fully recognized and treated, many men suffered the loss of toes or even feet caused by fungal infections that turned gangrenous. The problem did not entirely go away and was rather bad in Gallipoli but it was never again as severe as at the beginning of the war.

Venereal Diseases

Life in the trenches was most unpleasant and totally devoid of any sexual excitement. On returning to areas away from the war, in the little free time available, men's thoughts often returned to the normal pleasures of life. Who could blame them? They were living with the very real prospect of a violent death any day. Sex was often available for purchase from local ladies at a price. The financial price was not high perhaps because, with the number of men visiting each prostitute, and the very limited time given to each customer, the costs were kept down. There was often however another price to pay. Cleanliness was not a first priority of either party and venereal disease was quite common. Contraception in the form of condoms (known at the time as 'preventative outfits') was rare. Although some were issued to troops they were not popular. They were mostly heavy, hand-dipped items made from rubber cement. They were as thick as bicycle tyre inner tubes, uncomfortable to use and not very reliable. Brothels, official and otherwise, certainly existed, mostly in back areas and controlled to a degree by the French civilian authorities. French and German troops were permitted brothels whereas the British authorities did not officially organize them but generally adopted a pragmatic view of their existence. This periodically extended to the girls being inspected for disease by medical officers and for military police to control any queues that formed outside.

Table 7. Admissions for treatment for venereal disease	
Theatre of war	**Admissions**
France and Flanders	153,531
Other theatres of war	63,248
United Kingdom	199,719
Total	416,498

The figures in Table 7 for admissions for treatment for venereal disease generally include both British and Dominion soldiers and their officers. Some of the figures relate to relapses. The lower numbers from theatres of war other than the Western Front reflect the fewer troops posted there and also the relative lack of opportunity or prostitutes. The high incidence in the United Kingdom probably reflects the numbers of troops under training and away from the confines of their families for the first time. Additionally, soldiers home on leave may well have brought the previously undiagnosed disease back with them.

The figures combine gonorrhoea, syphilis and the various other venereal diseases. Overall, approximately four times as many cases of gonorrhoea were treated than syphilis. Without antibiotics, treatment was rather painful and, before 1910, fraught with dangers. It was discovered that syphilis could be treated with Salvarsan, an arsenical compound, otherwise known as '606'. The latter name was given as it was the 606th such compound to be tested. One famous Wimpole Street venereologist was even known among many officers as 'Dr 6-0-6' and, as a pragmatist, he gave his young nephew a small packet of it to take to France lest he should catch syphilis. Although gonorrhoea was perhaps less serious than syphilis, there was no effective treatment for it during the First World War. Attempts to cure it were however made by using quite toxic injections of silver nitrate or mercury. All treatments were very painful and had potentially dangerous side effects.

Various Notes and Medical Statistics

Whereas the precise cause of death was rarely investigated and recorded – beyond the term 'killed in action' – records were kept of the causes of injuries, including those that resulted in death. Statistics exist to show the ratio of battle to non-battle wounded. Battle was the result of enemy action. Non-battle was from all other causes such as sickness and accidents. The ratio of the latter varies considerably depending upon the theatre of war.

Table 8. British Expeditionary Forces: official statistics for admissions to hospitals		
France and Flanders	Battle	1,988,969
France and Flanders	Non-battle	3,528,486
All theatres of war	Battle	2,169,072
All theatres of war	Non-battle	6,186,767

However, more men were out of action through non-battle incidents than as a result of enemy action during the Great War.

The figures quoted in this book differentiate as far as possible between those already dead and those who reached medical aid still alive. That is not always easy, for the published figures are often blurred.

It will be seen from Table 8 that more were unavailable for duty through sickness or accidental injury than from enemy action. It must also be realized that the figures relate to occurrences of injury or sickness and not people. Some soldiers were wounded or sick several times. Indeed, nearly 11,000 men serving on 25 October 1917 had already been wounded three times or more. A good number of 'sick' were undoubtedly suffering from 'Spanish Flu'. All official figures seem to imply that all the casualties were men. That is not true. We must remember that women also served in theatres of war and many were killed or wounded.

Table 9 shows causes of wounds analysed at a casualty clearing station for the Director-General, Army Medical Services. The sample, at 212,659 cases, is relatively small but probably representative. It does not analyse those killed outright and it is possible that certain machines of war were more lethal than others. It clearly shows that the greatest killer was artillery fire.

Table 9. Analysis of causes of wounds seen at a casualty clearing station		
Wounding agent	**Number**	**%**
Bullet: rifle or machine gun	82,901	38.98
Shells, trench mortars, etc.	124,425	58.51
Bombs and grenades	4,649	2.19
Bayonet	684	0.32

The Germans recorded that 12 per cent of leg wounds and 23 per cent of arm wounds resulted in death, mainly through infection. The Americans recorded that 44 per cent of casualties that developed gangrene and half of those who were wounded in the head died.

Overall approximately 58 per cent of British wounded were treated and returned to duty in the theatre of war where the injury occurred. Around 38 per cent were evacuated overseas to recover. It is thought 82 per cent of injured or sick soldiers eventually returned to serve in the Army, even if in a less demanding unit than their original one.

War Pensions

Depending upon the severity of the injury, pensions were paid to wounded officers, men and nurses. By 31 March 1920 the number of awards had reached 1,182,368 but many pensions were only paid for a limited duration. The wives of severely disabled pensioners received a supplementary sum. In addition, nearly two million dependants, mostly comprising 232,254 widows and the children of the war dead, received a small pension. The majority of the dead were young unmarried men and it was extremely rare for their parents to receive any compensation from the state.

Chapter 10

INTERESTING FACTS, DEFINITIONS AND STATISTICS

First Casualties

In all probability the first British casualties from enemy action in the Great War occurred on 6 August 1914, less than thirty-two hours after the war started. HMS *Amphion* was engaged in action with the German minelayer *Königin Luise* in the North Sea. The enemy ship was sunk but the *Amphion*, having rescued some of her crew, ran over two of the mines laid by the *Königin Luise*. Some 150 British sailors were lost, together with several German prisoners.

First British Rifle Shots in Anger

On 22 August 1914, Corporal Ernest Thomas, 4th Irish Dragoon Guards, was on patrol on the Mons-Charlois Road in Belgium when a German cavalry patrol approached. Corporal Thomas, who came from Brighton in Sussex, fired upon the patrol at 400 yards range and hit a German officer.

First Royal Flying Corps Aircraft Shot Down

This occurred just after 10.16am on 22 August 1914 when an Avro 504 of 5 Squadron flown by Second Lieutenant Vincent Waterfall, with Lieutenant Charles Bayly as his observer, were on reconnaissance above Enghien. The observer's report (later recovered) recorded extensive enemy formations below. This transpired to be the 12th Brandenburg Volunteers, which shot the aeroplane down with rifle fire.

Armistice Day Fatalities

Sadly this day, 11 November 1918, several hundred servicemen throughout the whole British 'Empire' died from all causes – many of them from influenza. Of those, eight soldiers in the British Army were actually killed in action that morning. Private George Price, 28 Battalion Canadian Infantry, was also killed. It is thought he was the last soldier to be killed in action when he was shot dead by a sniper at two minutes to eleven – the hour appointed for the ceasefire. He is buried at St Symphorien Military Cemetery near Mons.

Duration of the War

This was the term that was applied on enlistment for general service in the regular army. Soldiers signed up for a number of years – usually three – or 'the duration of the War'. Sometimes the phrase used was 'until the War is over'.

With the Great War commencing at 11pm on 4 August 1914 (midnight Berlin time) and the Armistice taking effect at 11am on 11 November 1918, it lasted, on the Western Front, for 1,560 days. That is true for the British. The French and Belgians were at war a few days earlier. Many countries joined in, at least notionally, as the war progressed and the likely outcome became more certain.

The USA declared war on Germany on 6 April 1917 and on Austria-Hungary on 7 December 1917. It busied itself under the command of General John Joseph 'Black Jack' Pershing, building up its embryonic army with men and machines. With a few exceptions it did not get heavily involved in fighting until July 1918. Their biggest period of engagement was from 26 September 1918 until the end of the war. They did however sell war materials to the Allies from a much earlier date. And they bankrolled much of the war. Their greatest accomplishment was in their potential to supply both men and materials in huge quantities. The Germans knew this threat and realized they could never win once the American steamroller got under way. They considered they had one last chance and thus launched the Spring 1918 Offensives to pre-empt the involvement of America.

Theatres of War

These are based upon Army Order 391 of 1922, which supersedes earlier orders and was the criteria used to determine whether or not the Victory Medal should be granted (see Chapter 2). Essentially the operational areas are divided into seven regions. These in turn are subdivided and numbered accordingly. The numbering system changed slightly from 1 January 1916. Many soldiers in fact died in non-operational areas – sometimes, but by no means always, as the result of enemy action. The full text of Army Order 391 of 1922 is complex and most places listed have date qualifications added. These are omitted here for brevity. There were in addition other areas where deaths occurred. I have included these at the end of Table 10 and for uniformity I have continued with the run of numbers.

Table 10. Theatres of War	
1 Western European Theatre	France & Belgium and Italy.
2 Balkan Theatre	Greek Macedonia [Salonica], Serbia, Bulgaria, European Turkey, Gallipoli and islands of the Aegean Sea.
3 Russian Theatre	All operations.
4 Egyptian Theatre	Includes Palestine and Syria.
5 African Theatre	British East Africa, German East Africa, Portuguese East Africa, Rhodesia, Nyasaland and Uganda, German South West Africa, Cameroons, Nigeria, Togoland.
6 Asian Theatres	Hedjaz, Mesopotamia, Persia, South West Arabia, Aden, Frontier Regions [only] of India, Tsing-Tau (China).
7 Australasian Theatre	New Britain, New Ireland, Kaiser Wilhelm-Land, Admiralty Islands, Nauru, German Samoa.
8 Home	All those who died, from all causes, within the British Isles. Many were soldiers wounded overseas in an operational theatre who had been returned to Britain for treatment but succumbed to their injuries. Others died in Britain from illness or accident.
9 At sea	Mainly men on troop or hospital ships which sank. (Royal Navy rules differed from the Army.)
10 Other areas	Those who died in non-operational areas, including prisoners of war who died in captivity.

Strategy and Tactics

Strategic policy may be defined as the long-term objective of, for example, a war. The strategical policy of the Great War was to defeat the enemy and force him to leave occupied territory. How a strategic objective was achieved depended upon the tactics used. The decision to attempt a breakthrough on the Somme was a tactical move. By itself it could not realize the overriding strategical policy but was one of the many tactics used to achieve the goal.

Flak

Flieger Abwehr-Kanone (flak) was the German term for both anti-aircraft guns and the fire from guns designed or adapted for use against aircraft. The idea was not new. It began as early as 1846. By 1870 French balloons in the Franco-Prussian war were being shot down by flak. German anti-aircraft equipment was well developed and most formidable by 1915.

Britain also deployed large numbers of guns to defend important sites in Britain and on the Western Front but their overall success rate was very poor. Anti-aircraft guns were manned by the Royal Garrison Artillery from 1916. The accompanying searchlights were the responsibility of the Royal Engineers.

Calibre

This normally refers to the diameter of the hole (or bore) in the barrel of a gun. In military weapons it is usually measured in inches or millimetres or even in centimetres for large continental artillery pieces. As the bore had rifling groves cut in it, it is important to realize that there were two different measurements. This depends on whether one measures across the wider parts (grooves) or the narrower parts (lands). Unfortunately there is no 'industry standard' so it can be confusing. The British .303 is measured across the lands. If it were calculated across the grooves it would measure .311. In any event, the specified calibre is notional because manufacturing tolerances plus wear and tear result in varying gauge measurements. The differences and reasons are not of concern here.

Parachutes

It is true British aircrew were denied the 'luxury' of parachutes during the Great War. There does not seem to have been any official dictate that prohibited their use on the grounds that, if pilots had parachutes, they would not press home an attack but seek to bale out at the first opportunity. That story seems to be one of the many myths of war although there is some element of truth in it. The reality is a little more complicated.

By 1914 the development of parachutes was already progressing well. There were two main types. One was heavy and bulky and essentially consisted of an upturned container fixed to the side of a balloon basket. It contained a parachute that was attached by a primitive harness to the airman whilst aloft. All he had to do was jump and his weight pulled the parachute from the fixed container and deployed it. The other type was self-contained in a pack worn by the parachutist and opened with a pull or ripcord when required. The former were used during the Great War by observation balloon crews and saved many lives. They were totally unsuitable for aircraft use and the existence of these free-fall types was rapidly forgotten.

Attempts to interest high command in the self-contained parachute were made many times during the war by interested parties. It seems that each time the official on whose desk the letter landed had more pressing matters to consider. Generally he was a senior officer in the flying corps who had not personally seen combat and the effects of being shot down in flames. Besides, as was frequently pointed out, relatively few pilots and observers were in fact being killed. It was not judged of sufficient imperative to expend time and money on development of what was later realized was already quite a good parachute. And they were not prepared to sanction the purchase and issue of the existing model. It may not have been perfect but was certainly better than no parachute! Each approach was met with procrastination. The excuse sometimes given was that the pilots did not want them! Unfortunately I doubt if any combat pilots, as opposed to deskbound senior commanders, were ever asked. Various committees were eventually formed to consider parachutes for airmen but it took until September 1918 for an order for parachutes to be placed. In the event none were ever deployed in action by the Royal Air Force. German pilots were slightly more fortunate in that parachutes were made available to them by mid-1918. Besides the use by balloonists, the only British deployment of parachutes in the Great War was to drop a few spies behind enemy lines in 1917.

Pyrotechnics

Both sides fired vast numbers of flares and rockets to illuminate the battlefields at night and to signal their artillery that support was required. Flares were chemical illuminates generally fired from hand-held pistols and were in a variety of colours. White flares were mostly used to detect or deter approaching enemy patrols. Whenever sentries heard a strange noise the sky would rapidly be lit up. Complete stillness was the only way the intruder might escape detection.

Signalling by rockets was all very well but the observer could only respond to a prearranged code, depending upon which colour rocket was used. If the message was the usual SOS – meaning 'I need artillery support now' – that's fine, but what exactly does the artillery fire at? Like all communications in the First World War, signal rockets were of limited value.

France

France suffered many more war dead and wounded than Britain. The figures are analysed later. We must also remember it was land in France and Belgium where much of the fighting and destruction took place. See Table 11 for some recently published statistics for France.

Table 11. Destruction suffered in France	
Villages 100% destroyed	1,699
Villages 75% destroyed	707
Villages 50% destroyed	1,656
Houses completely destroyed	319,269
Houses partially destroyed	313,675
Factories destroyed	20,603
Railway track destroyed (kilometres)	7,985
Railway bridges destroyed	4,875
Railway tunnels destroyed	12
Roads destroyed (kilometres)	52,754
Non-cultivated land ruined (hectares)	2,060,000
Cultivated land ruined (hectares)	1,740,000

German Spies and their Fate

Prior to the war, Germany set up a spy network in Great Britain. This was discovered by the authorities and, when war started, most involved were arrested and interned. This effectively destroyed German espionage in Britain. Eleven further spies arrived after hostilities began but, because of their incompetence, were quickly discovered and arrested. All were tried and convicted and subsequently executed by firing squad at the Tower of London. The eleven men listed, with their dates of execution, were all buried in the East London cemetery at Plaistow.

Karl Hans Lody	6 November 1914
Karl T Muller	23 June 1915
Wilhelm Johannes Roos	30 July 1915
Haike Marius Petrus Janssen	30 July 1915
Ernst (or Emil) Waldermar Melin	10 September 1915
Agusto Alfredo Roggin	17 September 1915
Fernando Buschmann	19 October 1915
Georg T Breecknow	26 October 1915
Irving Guy Ries	27 October 1915
Albert Mayer	2 December 1915
Ludovico Zender y Hurwitz	11 April 1916

British Army Ranks 1914–1918

In the British Army, because of the peculiarities of the time some 'ranks', for example, lance-corporal, were classified as 'appointments'. Many of the lower ranks especially had traditional, comparable titles for men in non-infantry units. For example, both a sapper (Royal Engineers) and a gunner (Royal Artillery) were approximately equivalent in rank to a private. A bombardier in the Royal Artillery and a forewoman in Queen Mary's Army Auxiliary Corps were equivalent to a corporal.

At the non-commissioned officer (NCO)/warrant officer (WO) level there were many titles depending upon the branch of service and the job. Examples include: 'shoeing and carriage smith corporal', 'artificer lance-corporal', 'bandmaster', and 'armament quarter master sergeant'. Indeed, the supply and provision sections (the quartermasters of the army) had a whole plethora of ranks to themselves. The regimental sergeant-major was the senior warrant officer (first class) in a battalion responsible for discipline. Of equal rank, if perhaps not status, was the regimental quarter master sergeant.

Some units had interesting titles for various ranks. In the cavalry a corporal of the horse was equivalent to an infantry sergeant, a conductor in the Royal Army Ordnance Corps was a warrant officer (first class) and a nagsman was a private in the Army Service Corps. A list of ranks is given later.

Commissions during the war were most commonly temporary ones that would not continue much beyond the cessation of hostilities – hence the expression 'Temporary Gentlemen'. As a result of casualties, officers holding comparatively junior substantive ranks quite often held fairly senior posts temporarily, until regular army officers became available to fill those senior posts on a permanent basis. There were no temporary gentlemen appointed on a substantive basis to command brigades and above. For examples of the jobs held by different ranks see Chapter 2. Table 12 shows comparative ranks for officers with the Royal Navy. From its inception on 1 April 1918 until after the end of the Great War, the Royal Air Force used the same rank names as the army.

Table 12. Ranks of officers in the Army and Royal Navy	
Army	**Royal Navy**
Field Marshal	Admiral of the Fleet
General	Admiral
Lieutenant-General	Vice-Admiral
Major-General	Rear-Admiral
Brigadier-General	Commodore
Colonel	Captain
Lieutenant-Colonel	Commander
Major	Lieutenant-Commander
Captain	Lieutenant
Lieutenant	Sub Lieutenant
Second Lieutenant	

Using *Soldiers Died in the Great War* as a source, it is possible to identify well over 100 different army 'ranks' of men and women who perished in the conflict and these are listed below in their main groupings.

Warrant Officers

Armament Sergeant Major, Bandmaster, Battery Sergeant Major, Company Sergeant Major, Conductor, Corporal Major, Drill Sergeant, Farrier Sergeant Major, Machinist Sergeant Major, Master Gunner (WO I), Master Gunner 1st class, Master Gunner 2nd class, Orderly Room Quarter Master Sergeant, Regimental Quarter Master Sergeant, Regimental Sergeant Major, Sergeant Major, Squadron Corporal Major, Staff Sergeant Major, Sub-Conductor, Superintending Clerk Transport Sergeant Major, Warrant Officer, Warrant Officer Class I, Warrant Officer Class II, Wheeler Quarter Master Sergeant.

Sergeants

Armament Quarter Master Sergeant, Armourer Staff Sergeant, Band Sergeant, Battery Quarter Master Sergeant, Bugler Major, Bugler Sergeant, Colour Sergeant, Company Quarter Master Sergeant, Cook Sergeant, Corporal of Horse, Drummer Sergeant, Farrier Corporal of Horse, Farrier Quarter Master Sergeant, Farrier Sergeant, Farrier Staff Sergeant, Fitter Sergeant, Fitter Staff Sergeant, Flight Cadet, Lance Sergeant, Orderly Room Sergeant, Piper Sergeant, Quarter Master Sergeant, Saddler Quarter Master Sergeant, Saddler Sergeant, Saddler Staff Sergeant, Saddle-Tree Maker Sergeant, Sergeant, Shoeing Smith Sergeant, Signaller Sergeant, Squadron Quarter Master Corporal, Staff Sergeant, Trumpeter Sergeant, Wheeler Quarter Master Sergeant, Wheeler Sergeant, Wheeler Staff Sergeant, Wheelwright Sergeant.

Corporals

Artificer Corporal, Artificer Lance Corporal, Bombardier, Corporal, Farrier Corporal, Farrier Staff Corporal, Fitter Corporal, Forewoman, Lance Bombardier, Lance Corporal, Saddler Corporal, Shoeing and Carriage Smith Corporal, Shoeing Smith Corporal, Signaller Bombardier, Signaller Corporal, Signaller Lance Bombardier, Smith Corporal, Wheeler Corporal.

Privates

Armourer, Artificer, Band Boy, Bandsman, Boy, Bugler, Cadet, Cyclist, Driver, Farrier, Fitter, Guardsman, Gunner, Motor Cyclist, Musician, Nagsman, Piper, Private, Rifleman, Rough Rider, Saddler, Sapper, Shoeing & Carriage Smith, Shoeing Smith, Signaller, Strapper, Tailor, Trooper, Trumpeter, Waggoner, Wheeler, Wheelwright, Worker.

See Table 13 for ranks in the Indian Army and Table 14 for selected ranks in the German Army.

Table 13. Indian Army ranks 1914-1918 (Infantry)	
Viceroy's Commissioned Officers	
Subadar-Major	
Subadar	No British Army equivalents
Jemadar	
Other Ranks	
Havildar-Major	Company Sergeant-Major
Havildar	Sergeant
Naik	Corporal
Lance-Naik	Lance-Corporal
Sepoy	Private

Table 14. Selected German Army Ranks 1914-1918	
Armierungssoldat	Armourer
Fahrer	Driver
Feldwebel	Company Sergeant-Major
Füsilier	Rifleman
Gefreiter	Lance-Corporal
Grenadier	Bomber
Hauptmann	Captain
Infanterist	Infantry soldier
Jäger	Rifleman
Kanonier	Gunner

Table 14 - *continued*

Landsturmmann	Storm-trooper
Leutnant	Second Lieutenant
Major	Major
Musketier	Private
Oberleutnant	Lieutenant
Oberst	Colonel
Oberstleutnant	Lieutenant-Colonel
Pionier	Pioneer
Reservist	Reservist
Rittmeister	Captain (Cavalry)
Schütze	Sniper or Marksman
Sergeant	Senior Non Commissioned Officer
Soldat	Soldier/private
Telegraphist	Telegraphist
Ulan	Cavalryman
Unteroffizier	Non Commissioned Officer

Stores

War is a costly business and not just in respect of the human and animal lives lost or injured. The following few figures give us just a small picture of the logistical problem of supplying the 'men at the front'. Table 15 shows stores shipped to France, for use on the Western Front alone, during the war. There were many other items and altogether over 25 million tons were shipped.

To give some small idea of what all this represents, Table 16 shows some items purchased for the army in 1918 alone. This is but a small sample. There were many more items of equipment, etc. With cigarettes at the time of the Great War being much smaller than they are now, and without a filter tip, this represents rather a lot of cigarettes. No wonder so many pictures of soldiers show them with either a pipe or cigarette in their mouths.

Table 15. Stores shipped to France during the war	
Supply	**Weight in tons**
Food	3,240,948
Fodder (oats and hay)	5,438,602
Coal	3,922,391
Ammunition	9,438,614
Ordnance (artillery pieces)	1,761,777
Petrol and sundries	758,614
Royal Engineer stores (general)	1,369,894
Railway material	988,354

Note: The difference between approximate imperial and metric tons (tonnes) is negligible for the purposes of this table.

Table 16. Some items purchased for the Army in 1918	
Biscuits	129,204,000lbs (58,606,549kg)
Margarine	52,203,000lbs (23,679,125kg)
Sugar	167,234,000lbs (75,856,844 kg)
Meat and vegetable rations	38,262,000 tins
Preserved meat (Bully beef)	168,745,000 tins
Tobacco and cigarettes	14,409,000lbs (6,535879kg)

To help with the supply of meat, shortages of which were occurring due to losses in shipping caused by enemy submarines, rabbits were introduced as an occasional substitute early in 1917. During the remainder of the war 5,649,797 rabbit skins were sold to help with the costs. Many women of the time wore rabbit skin (marketed as coney) fur coats.

Women on the Western Front

In August 1918 the following numbers of women were recorded as being on the Western Front: Royal Army Medical Corps (all grades, British, Colonial and American) 7,123; British Red Cross Society (nursing sisters and other workers) 1,094; Queen Mary's Army Auxiliary Corps 7,808; YMCA, Church Army, Salvation Army, other institutions 1,056; General Service Voluntary Aid Detachments (VAD, drivers) 99. Of these, 302 were to die, including 45 as a direct result of enemy action.

Boring But Important Statistics

The figures shown below are derived, wherever possible, from official sources. These include: *Statistics of the Great War, Official Histories, Hansard* (5 May 1921), *Soldiers Died in the Great War* and the Commonwealth War Graves Commission.

Unfortunately there are many official sources, no two of which seem to agree. Indeed the official *Statistics of the Great War* sometimes shows different figures for apparently the same criteria on different pages! This is a compilation using the figures most likely to be accurate. We must realize that different sources use different criteria. Often they do not show clearly who is included or excluded or for what precise period. Again, whether or not all theatres of war are included is often shrouded in mystery. For many events, especially early in the war, few records were kept. Reasonably accurate statistics did not start until October 1916. Because of the very nature of war the record keeping was not precise. Sometimes records were lost or deliberately destroyed. Many men simply disappeared without trace. Unless otherwise specified, the figures relate solely to British personnel. Sometimes however they include British, Dominion, Commonwealth and Colonial Forces. In that case the term 'Commonwealth' is used as an indicator.

Please use all these statistics with the 'health warning' attributed to Benjamin Disraeli who once said, 'there are three kinds of lies: lies, damned lies, and statistics'! We must also remember that, although the Armistice took effect on 11 November 1918, that did not mean the end to all conflict. It was the cessation of hostilities on the Western Front. But it took a while for the message that it was over to reach far-flung operations. And fighting continued in Russia between the Allies and the Bolsheviks until the final withdrawal on 12 October 1919.

Additionally, men still died of wounds, disease or accidents after the Armistice and indeed sometimes long after the official casualty lists had closed. Variations will also occur as, for example, deaths were often not recorded until after the fateful event and in consequence the wrong date attributed. For the First World War the Commonwealth War Graves Commission's records run from 4 August 1914 to 31 August 1921.

Table 17. Overall mobilization and losses figures

Country	Mobilized	Military deaths	Wounded[a]
British Forces[b]	9,496,170[c]	989,075	2,121,906[d]
France	8,410,000	1,385,300[e]	4,266,000
Italy	5,615,000	462,391	953,886
Russia	12,000,000	1,700,000	4,950,000
United States	4,355,000[f]	115,660[g]	205,690
Germany	11,000,000	1,808,545	4,247,143[h]
Austro-Hungary	7,800,000	1,200,000	3,620,000[i]
Turkey	2,850,000	325,000	400,000

Note: The figures are based upon War Office statistics and do not include civilian deaths during or after the war, regardless of cause.

[a] Number of times wounded, not necessarily the number of men. Many men were wounded more than once.

[b] All British and Commonwealth forces.

[c] Includes all arms, e.g. army, naval and air services, plus women's services. Not all saw active service and many remained at home. Of the total, 8,586,202 served in the army.

[d] An additional 196,318 Commonwealth all ranks were reported as prisoners of war or interned in neutral countries. Of these 16,402 died in captivity.

[e] It is thought around 400,000 French colonial troops also perished in the war.

[f] Of these, nearly 2 million had arrived in France before the Armistice.

[g] Of these around 51,000 relate to deaths in battle, i.e. killed in action or died of wounds.

[h] In addition about 1 million German officers and men were captured and became prisoners of war. During 6 Aug.–11 Nov. 1918 (the last '100' days) 186,684 enemy prisoners were captured on the Western Front.

[i] Another 2 million Austro-Hungarian servicemen became prisoners of war.

Table 17 shows the numbers of people mobilized and of losses. The total estimated population in the British Isles at July 1914 was 46,331,548. By the end of the war Germany had 3,403,000 men, both combat and otherwise, available on the Western Front with more in other theatres of war and at Home. To oppose them Britain mustered 1,731,578, France 2,562,000 and the

USA 1,924,000 men respectively on the Western Front. Not all of these were combatants.

The word 'strength' was officially defined as follows. Ration strength was the total number of men (excluding coloured labour and prisoners of war) who were being fed from Army stocks in France (and Belgium). Combatant strength was all fighting troops (infantry, cavalry, artillery, and engineer field units), together with the troops in divisional or base depots. Rifle strength was officers and men in infantry battalions alone. The following numbers, for 11 November 1918, are very different from those in Table 18 and we must remember only apply to France and Belgium: ration strength 1,731,578, combatant strength 1,164,790, rifle strength 461,748.

Table 18. Estimated strength of British Army (only) personnel (including Territorial Force, and regular reservists)		
Officers	4 August 1914	28,060
	11 November 1918	164,255
Other ranks	4 August 1914	708,618
	1 November 1918	3,595,216

Note: Included in the totals for Nov. 1918 were 1,514,933 officers and men in various medical categories retained in Britain.

Table 19 shows the estimated British air strength. There were, in addition, vast quantities of spares including 22,171 airframes and 37,702 engines! This, no doubt, is the reason for the often-quoted number of 20,000 aircraft available to the Royal Air Force in November 1918. Table 20 gives the figures for the Royal Navy.

Table 19. Estimated strength of British air services (all branches that served during the war)		
Officers	August 1914	276
	November 1918	27,333
Other ranks	August 1914	1,797
	November 1918	263,842
First-line strength in aircraft		
August 1914	50 aeroplanes and seaplanes, 6 airships	
November 1918	3,300 aeroplanes and seaplanes, 103 airships.	

Table 20. Estimated strength of the Royal Navy (all branches that served during the war)

Officers	15 July 1914	9,986
	Commissioned or entered service during the war	45,391
Other ranks	15 July 1914	136,061
	Mobilized or entered service during the war:	448,799

Major British warships[a]	4 Nov. 1914	Ships lost[b]	11 Nov. 1918
Battleships: Dreadnoughts	20	13[c]	33
Pre-Dreadnoughts	40		29
Battlecruisers	9	3	9
Cruisers and light cruisers	108	19	129
Torpedo boat destroyers	215	64	407
Aircraft carriers[d]	1	3	13
Submarines	76	54	137

[a] Details from *Official History (Naval Operations)*
[b] Includes not only ships sunk – some deliberately as blockships – but also others which were scrapped, assigned to other navies, or converted to depot ships etc. during the war.
[c] Battleship losses include pre-Dreadnoughts.
[d] The aircraft carriers might more properly be described as seaplane carriers.

Table 21 includes all causes of death (e.g. killed in action, died of wounds or otherwise died from causes which may or may not have involved enemy action, such as accident, disease or drowning). It must be realized that the vast majority of men in the Royal Navy who died were technically drowned, but this was usually as a result of enemy action.

For the figures listed for the air services, 43 per cent were killed in action or died of wounds; 32 per cent were killed or died as a result of flying accidents etc. and 25 per cent died from other causes. For full details of all British and Commonwealth air service casualties, and a lot more, see *Airmen Died in the Great War* by Chris Hobson.

The figures concerning the Army are an amalgam of causes approximately attributable to the three main groupings – killed in action, died of wounds (both attributable to enemy action) and died, which applies to non-battle casualties. For example, in the non-battle casualties are included over 283 army officers and men known to have drowned by misfortune. The fatal casualties also includes those who died, other than in

Table 21. Deaths in the British armed forces during the Great War			
British Army (excluding Royal Flying Corps)			
Cause of death	**Officers**	**Other ranks**	**Totals**
Killed in action	27,444 (70%)	437,872 (66%)	465,316 (66%)
Died of wounds	8,508 (22%)	137,935 (21%)	146,443 (21%)
Died	3,318 (8%)	86,153 (13%)	89,471 (13%)
Total	39,270	661,960	701,230
Royal Navy			
		Officers	3,279
		Other ranks	36,533
		Total	39,812
Royal Naval Division			
		Officers	463
		Other ranks	8,127
		Total	8,590
Air Services[a]			
		Officers	6,059
		Other ranks	3,069
		Total	9,128
Officers and men in the British Mercantile Marine			14,879
Officers and men of British Fishing Vessels			434

[a] Royal Flying Corps, Royal Naval Air Service and Royal Air Force.

action, in the United Kingdom and overseas, perhaps from accident or disease.

On average 634 British and Commonwealth service personnel were killed every day of the Great War. The British Army alone lost, on average, 450 each day. Overall, on all sides, one person perished about every ten seconds.

The Commonwealth War Graves Commission shows the following figures in its Annual Report for 2007. The figures are for Great War servicemen and women from the United Kingdom and Colonies, Undivided India, Canada, Australia, New Zealand and South Africa.

Identified war burials	587,684
Unidentified war burials	187,853
Total number of graves	775,537
Commemorated on memorials	526,974

Examination of these figures reveals the stark truth that, despite the best endeavours, vast numbers of British and Commonwealth bodies remain to this day where they fell – be it on land or sea. They are not alone, for there are also many hundreds of thousands of soldiers, sailors and airmen from other nations who fought and died in the Great War and who have no known grave. They are all still missing.

Table 22. British military deaths from all causes by year

	Officers	Other ranks	Totals
1914 (5 Aug.–31 Dec.)	1,465	25,421	26,886
1915	5,694	107,408	113,102
1916	9,125	161,057	170,182
1917	11,079	189,528	200,607
1918 (to 11 Nov.)	10,886	174,266	185,152
Other periods	1,021	4,280	5,301
Totals	39,270	661,960	701,230

Table 23. Miscellaneous statistics for the Army

Soldiers only	Killed in action	Died of wounds	Died
Western European theatre	404,255	120,890	34,284
United Kingdom	20	6,167	26,369
Other theatres	33,597	10,878	25,500
Total	437,872	137,935	86,153
Total of British other ranks who lost their lives in the Great War			661,960

Table 24. Deaths from all causes in various different branches of the army			
Corps etc	**Officers**	**Other ranks**	**Totals**
Cavalry (total)	1,047	8,727	9,774
Artillery (RFA)	2,511	30,451	32,962
Artillery (RGA)	894	12,749	13,643
(Total Artillery)	(3,405)	(43,200)	(46,605)
Medical Corps	709	5,538	6,247
Royal Engineers	1,165	16,125	17,290
Army Service Corps	410	8,050	8,462

Table 25. Deaths of Commonwealth service personnel	
Country	**Total Service Deaths**
Canada	64,962
Newfoundland	1,204
Australia	61,927
New Zealand	18,051
Undivided India	74,190
South Africa	9,474
Other colonies	507
Total	230,315

Attrition

When taking into account the casualties in all armed forces who died from any cause, plus those missing, wounded, or made prisoner of war, approximately 52.3 per cent of all Allied forces became casualties compared with 57.5 per cent of enemy forces. What none of these statistics reveal, however, is the immense suffering endured by the victim before oblivion intervened. I doubt many truly died instantaneously.

Chapter 11

A GUIDE TO VISITING THE WESTERN FRONT BATTLEFIELDS

Having read about the Great War and maybe seen pictures, films or videos, the next step surely is to visit some of the battlefields. It really is simple. You can use the services of a specialist travel company or go on your own. The principle is no different from taking any other kind of holiday.

This is not a conventional annual guidebook and so I am not recommending any particular places to stay or eat as they can easily go out of business or change in quality over the years. It is far better to consult a good travel agent or surf the internet to find somewhere to suit your taste. What I am offering are sensible travel tips and advice commensurate with travel on the Western Front. Please do not think that the First World War only concerned the Ypres Salient with Passchendaele or the Somme. There is so much more to see. Why not visit Neuve Chapelle, or the Loos battlefields, or Cambrai, or indeed any of the battlefields where British soldiers fought and died? A list of battles appears at the end of this chapter. The French battlefields and museums around Verdun are also well worth visiting and give some idea of the huge sacrifices made by our allies.

Getting There

The main areas of the Western Front are very easy to reach and your motoring organization can supply not only the best route but inform of any current disruptions likely to cause delay. The easiest ways to cross the English Channel are by ferry or the Channel Tunnel. Quite frankly, any time of year is good to visit the area for each season has its own attractions and disadvantages.

Suggested Kit List

The most important items are of course your passport, travel documents, euros and a credit card. You should also carry your EHIC (European Health Insurance Card) that offers limited medical cover in the European Community. It is additionally highly advisable to have a separate comprehensive holiday insurance policy.

If you are driving then be sure to take your driving licence, insurance certificate – endorsed for overseas use – and the vehicle's registration document. You are required to adjust your headlamp beams to suit driving on the right on the continent, even if you only intending to drive in daylight hours. Compulsory accessories include a breakdown warning triangle, a spare set of bulbs, a first aid kit and a high-visibility jacket for each occupant. I recommend a vehicle recovery insurance that will repatriate passengers and car and supply a loan car in event of breakdown. Motoring organizations have various policies on offer. It is always best to check the latest driving regulations, including essential car accessories, before starting out. Laws and regulations change and do not always mirror those in the United Kingdom.

Most personal items, left at home in error, can be purchased overseas. The amount and extent of luggage you take will depend upon the type of accommodation chosen and the amount of time you plan to spend there. There are however several extra items which may be useful and increase your enjoyment.

A good guidebook for the area you are visiting.

Overview and local maps.

Perhaps a GPS or similar device and a compass. (See separate section on trench maps.)

Suitable warm/cool weatherproof clothing and footwear depending on the season.

Notebook and pencil.

All-weather ballpoint pen (for signing cemetery registers).

Torch – always useful.

Camera, plus spare batteries and films or memory cards.

Binoculars.

Water bottle. It can be very thirsty work exploring the battlefields.

202 • The Great War Handbook

Useful Telephone Numbers

Throughout the European Union the general emergency number is 112. It works equally well in the United Kingdom. If you are using a mobile phone it is simplest and generally best to use this number for any emergency service within the European Union. Even if you have no credit or SIM card in your phone, it will work for the 112 designated emergency number. Most operators speak English.

In France the quickest response to a medical emergency is by dialling the fire brigade (Pompiers) who will despatch a competent medical team. Separate emergency numbers for France are: medical (Samu) 15, police 17, emergency medical aid or fire (Pompier) 18. In Belgium the numbers for fire or ambulance are 100 and for police 101.

The numbers for British Embassies etc. are:

Foreign and Commonwealth Office – London ++ 44 (0) 207 008 1500
British Embassy – Paris, France   ++ 33 (0) 1 44 51 31 00
British Consul – Lille, France   ++ 33 (0) 3 20 12 82 72
British Embassy – Brussels, Belgium   ++ 32 (0) 2 287 62 11

The initial two digits in international dialling can vary in different parts of the world. Consequently the international codes are frequently shown as: ++ followed by the country code. Here we are only considering calls between the United Kingdom, France and Belgium. Within those countries the initial access codes are currently: 00. Therefore dial for:

United Kingdom 00 44 (followed by national number – but see below)
France   00 33 (followed by national number – but see below)
Belgium   00 32 (followed by national number – but see below)

When dialling the United Kingdom from France or Belgium enter 00 44 then dial the full UK number *but omit* the leading (0) (zero). Thus, if you wanted to call 01234 567899 from France or Belgium dial: 00 44 1234 567899. With mobile phones you can generally just dial the usual number and the system will sort out where you are calling. If that does not work treat your mobile as a landline and enter the full international access codes, then omit the leading (0) zero but enter the remainder of the national number.

For tourist information contact:

French Tourist Board, Lincoln House, 300 High Holborn, London WC1V 7JH (tel. 09068 244 123): http://uk.franceguide.com/
Belgian Tourist Office, Innovation Centre, 225 Marsh Wall, London E14 9FW (tel. 0800-954 5245): http://www.visitbelgium.com/

Language

There are many differences between Belgium and France and language is just one element. Belgium is a small but vibrant country that is anxious to be involved in international commerce and world affairs. In consequence most modern Belgians speak several languages, with English being the most frequent second language. That said, many farmers and others from rural areas near the Ypres Salient only speak and understand Flemish. Conversation can occasionally be complicated!

The French are very proud of their culture, traditions and language and in France English is not so widely spoken. One may be lucky and find a friendly soul to help out, but do not presume. Finding that the waiter in the hotel speaks English is one thing but trying to explain exactly what you are doing to an irate French farmer who does not speak English can be quite another. It is also rare to find a French gendarme or police officer conversant in English. A little French can go a long way and be very useful on the battlefields and in the towns.

If all else fails, smiling, whilst reaching for the phrase book, often helps. Always be polite and friendly, as a guest in another country.

Recommended Guidebooks

There are, in addition to the short general list below, many specialist books concentrating upon specific battles and areas of conflict. The Battleground Europe series of guides published by Pen & Sword Books Ltd covers many of the areas on the Western Front and are well worth reading. An up-to-date list can be obtained from the publishers of this book. Guidebooks are notorious for becoming rapidly out of date, especially regarding accommodation and popular tourist attractions. Always check you have a recent edition.

General Books

Coombs, Rose E. *Before Endeavours Fade* (London: Battle of Britain Prints international Ltd – many editions). This is still one of the best single-volume guidebooks available.

Holt, Major Tonie and Mrs Valmai. various battlefield guides, for example:
Battlefield Guide to the Somme (Pen & Sword, 1996)
Battlefield Guide, Ypres Salient (Pen & Sword, 1997)
Battlefield Guide to the Western Front – North (Pen & Sword, 2004)

Battlefield Guide to the Western Front – South (Pen & Sword, 2005)

Detailed maps are included within each book and in the Somme and Ypres Salient editions separate maps are included which give a good overview and much more besides.

Walking Guides

Reed, Paul. *Walking the Somme* (Pen & Sword, 1997)
Reed, Paul. *Walking the Salient* (Pen & Sword, 1999)
Reed, Paul. *Walking Arras* (Pen & Sword 2007)
These are essential companions when walking the areas covered.

Maps

It is worth noting that many place names we are familiar with are not spelt the same in their own country. For example Dunkirk is spelt Dunkerque and Ypres is now Ieper. A grid showing maps for both France and Belgium can be obtained from the Institut Geographique National (IGN) or Nationaal Geografisch Instituut (NGI) or viewed on the internet.

France

By far the best to take are the IGN series. For a good overview and general driving (includes parts of Belgium): 1:250,000 scale (1cm = 2.5km), IGN RO1 Nord-Pas-de-Calais, Picardie. For more local detail, in 1:100,000 scale (1cm = 1km) IGN maps numbered from 01 to 10 cover the main battlefields but these two are especially useful.

    Map 02 Lille – Dunkerque (Dunkirk to Arras and including the Ypres Salient)

    Map 04 Laon – Arras (includes the Somme, St Quentin and Amiens)

Much more detail can be seen on the IGN 1:25 000 series (1cm = 250m). There are many covering the battlefields and it is worth consulting the latest catalogue from IGN before purchasing the ones for your chosen area.

Belgium

I recommend similar maps by NGI. These maps have a different numbering sequence and, for the Salient, the area is covered by Sheet 28. The area is subdivided and sections may be purchased in 1:50,000 or 1:20,000 scales. At 1:20,000 scale, the sections within Sheet 28 (using current spellings of Belgian towns) are:

28: 1–2   Poperinge–Ieper
28: 3–4   Zonnebeke–Moorslede
28: 5–6   Heuvelland–Mesen
28: 7–8   Wervik–Menen

You may also require sections within other sheets for other parts of Belgium.

As an alternative to IGN/NGI maps, Michelin make excellent maps for France and Belgium in various scales.

First World War Trench Maps

These are the maps, prepared during the course of the war, usually at 1:10,000 or 1:20,000 scale, showing not only the usual features but also with the enemy trench systems superimposed. Some maps also show and name the British trenches. British trench lines are shown in blue and German ones in red. That is until mid-1918 when, to conform to the French system, the situation was reversed. Thereafter British and Allied trenches were in red and the enemy trenches in blue. Check with the map date and key to verify which identification is in use. The method of pinpointing a map reference on trench maps is different to that in use today. It is explained, usually with examples, on each trench map or digital version and a few minutes learning the principle used would be advantageous. War diaries often quote map references and it is very useful to be able to locate the positions quoted on a trench map. Original maps are collectors' items and rather expensive but there are alternatives. It is possible to purchase photocopies of the desired area from the Imperial War Museum or from the Western Front Association.

Digital Mapping

Perhaps better still are the CD or DVD versions available which contain a very good selection of maps that can be printed – and in case of the DVD, with so much more besides. Before buying any digital item check it is compatible with your computer system. One thing about paper trench maps is that they do not 'crash' or become out of date!

There is now a system called LinesMan that incorporates around 750 scanned trench maps at 1:10,000 scale, plus sections of current French IGN maps at 1:25,000 scale, along with aerial photographs that cover much of the Western Front. Modern Belgian NGI maps are now also incorporated. It is possible to view any desired area on a computer and, if required, see two different maps side by side. Additionally any map can be viewed in 3-D that enables one to see the exact lie of the land. The features it incorporates are truly amazing and it revolutionizes trench mapping. Perhaps its greatest attribute is the ability to download maps to a hand-held GPS device and then plot your precise position whilst on the battlefields. This can be seen superimposed on either the trench maps or modern maps. I have used it 'in action' and highly recommend it.

Visiting the Battlefields

The swathes of land taken over by the trench systems of the First World War were, and still are, valuable agricultural fields. As soon as the war finished the farmers returned to their land and attempted to restore it to a pre-war state. They were not interested in preserving the legacy of the war. Today, most of the land fought over remains in private ownership and the farmers do not take kindly to their crops being trampled by visitors – most especially without prior permission.

It does not mean however that little remains to be seen on the public parts of the Western Front. Far from it. And most can be accessed easily and legally. Apart from visible scars on the landscape there are many museums and preserved sights to visit. There are areas however that cannot be reached by road or public path and it is here that the use of binoculars may help you avoid trespassing. Using the extract from the Battles Nomenclature Committee report of 1921, shown at the end of this chapter, you will get some idea as to the extent of the fighting on the Western Front. It shows only the places and years involved. Many were fought over more than once and reference to the *Official History of the War: Military Operations: France and Belgium* or other good history books will flesh out the details of the battles. The list, together with maps, gazetteers and guidebooks, can be used as a pointer to places to study and visit. There are so many worthwhile places to see and a little research will make your journey so much more rewarding.

There are literally thousands of cemeteries on the Western Front where British and Commonwealth soldiers lie buried. No visit to the battlefields can be complete without visiting some to remember the brave men and women who perished in the Great War. There are also many French, Belgian, American and German cemeteries, as well as those dedicated to other nationalities. It was British policy that every man should either have an individually named grave or be commemorated by name near to where he fell on one of several memorials constructed on the battlefields. Many bodies were recovered but not identified and were buried alongside their comrades. Those graves bear the mark *Known Unto God* and show as much information as possible, but all too frequently they simply state, *A Soldier of the Great War*. I have deliberately not suggested any particular cemeteries. It is for you to choose. The smaller cemeteries and the areas set aside in communal cemeteries contain a Cross of Sacrifice. Larger cemeteries also have a large Stone of Remembrance. Aside from smaller burial sites the graves are arranged in plots and then usually in uniform rows. Reference to an individual grave is by plot (if

Grave of unknown British soldier.

more than one), then by row and finally by grave number from the beginning of the row. For example the grave reference for Lieutenant Henry Webber, who died of wounds aged 68 and is buried in Dartmoor Cemetery, Becordel-Becourt is: I.G.54 (Plot 1, Row G, Grave 54).

The British and Commonwealth graves are beautifully tended by gardeners of the Commonwealth War Graves Commission and are a credit to that wonderful organization. When visiting any cemetery please respect the dead and do not mark a gravestone in any way to try and improve photography. They can be photographed quite adequately by shading the camera from the sun and/or choosing a slightly angled shot. It may sometimes be necessary to return at a better time of day when the light is more appropriate. Flash does not usually work as it obliterates any contrast. It is perfectly acceptable to place a poppy cross or wreath in front of a grave and then sign the visitors book found in the unlocked safe at most larger cemeteries or memorials. That safe

Grave of unknown German soldier.

usually contains a copy of the cemetery register. It is for all to use and must not be taken away.

If in the Ypres Salient and time permits I suggest you go to the Menin Gate in good time for the Last Post ceremony that takes place every night of the year at 8pm. It is very moving and really brings home the great sacrifice made by so many. Please just stand silently, respectfully and observe. Despite their excellence, do not applaud the buglers from the town fire service – it is not appropriate.

Guidebooks will show precise locations of sites and suggest tours within your chosen area but there are a few places one should really not miss and are well worth incorporating into your itinerary. We must also remember that there were other areas where British soldiers fought and died – for example on the Marne and the Aisne. In addition there are literally hundreds of miles of front where our brave allies, the Belgians and French were solely responsible. The Verdun battlefields alone took hundreds of thousands of lives and there is much to see there. Alas space permits only brief details of a few places. There are many more.

Belgium (Ypres Salient)

• Talbot House, Poperinghe: Its 'Everyman's Club' was started in 1915 by Reverend 'Tubby' Clayton as a rest home for soldiers going to and from the front. Famous for the 'Upper Room' – a tranquil chapel on the top floor, its hospitality and motto, 'abandon rank all ye who enter here'. (Visitor toilets available.)

• St Georges Memorial Church, Ypres: A very moving British church containing many memorials to the dead.

• Menin Gate: An imposing arched gateway to Ypres that commemorates by name nearly 55,000 soldiers with no known grave who died in the area before 15 August 1917. A further 35,000, who died after that date, are commemorated on the walls around Tyne Cot Cemetery.

• Hill 60: A preserved area where much tunnelling and fighting took place throughout most of the war. Many dead are still beneath it. Caterpillar mine crater is adjacent.

• Spanbroekmolen (Pool of Peace): The largest crater resulting from the mines blown on 7 June 1917 to open the Messines offensive.

• Sanctuary Wood: Preserved trenches now in private ownership. (Customer toilets available.)

France

• Thiepval Memorial: The largest memorial on the Western Front commemorating over 72,000 named soldiers with no known grave who died in the Somme region. There is a visitors' centre near to the memorial. (Visitor toilets available.)

• Vimy Ridge and Canadian Memorial: An area of preserved trenches and tunnels. The outstanding memorial commemorates 11,000 Canadian soldiers with no known grave who died in the First World War. (Visitor toilets available.)

• La Boisselle Mine Crater: An enormous crater resulting from the mine exploded on 1 July 1916. Unlike the craters in Belgium this one is dry

Thiepval Memorial to the Missing of the Somme.

and the full extent of its size can be appreciated from its rim. It is in private ownership but can be freely visited.

• Ulster Tower: In the heart of the Somme it contains a small museum and is dedicated to the memory of the Ulstermen who died in the Great War. (Customer toilets available.)

• Newfoundland Park: An area of preserved trenches, which gives some idea of the systems in place for the Battle of the Somme. It especially commemorates the men from Newfoundland, which was not part of Canada at the time. (Visitor toilets available.)

• Arras: There is an important memorial here to the missing of the region. It is attached to the Faubourg d'Amiens Commonwealth War Graves Cemetery and includes a separate memorial to missing airmen. Also at Arras is a new underground tunnel system in the Wellington Quarry, dug largely by New Zealand tunnellers and intended to shelter thousands of soldiers prior to the Battle of Arras. (Visitor toilets available.)

Museums

There are many municipal and private museums and a visit to the local *mairie* (town hall) will often reveal their whereabouts. Before visiting it is advisable to check the opening hours and cost and indeed if it is still there, as museums come and go! All museums vary in content, specialization and presentation. Some may appeal to you more than others. A few of the larger, and excellent museums in Belgium are:

In Flanders Fields Museum. The Cloth Hall, Ieper [Ypres]. (Visitors toilets available.)
Hooge Crater Museum, Old Chapel, Meenseweg 467-8902 (Menin Road), Zillebeke. (Customer toilets available.)
Dugout Experience. Ieperstraat 5, B-8980 Zonnebeke. (Visitor toilets available.)

And in France:

Historial de la Grande Guerre, Péronne. (Visitor toilets available.)
Musée des Abris, outside Basilique, Albert. (Nearby toilets available.)
Notre Dame de Lorette.

Metal Detectors

Do not take a metal detector with you. It is against the law to use them in most of the First World War battlefields. It is now also an offence to remove artefacts, however found, from the battlefields without official sanction and this law can be rigorously enforced. A good policy is that suggested at many world heritage sights. 'Take only photographs. Leave only footprints' – and even then be careful neither to photograph any current military installations nor to trespass.

Munitions Seen on the Battlefields

The first and only rule is: leave them alone! During the Great War the belligerents fired many hundreds of millions of shells of varying calibres and types. The British alone fired over 170 million shells – many containing poison gas. There were also many more hundreds of millions of grenades, mortar bombs and other lethal devices used in the fighting. Many millions failed to explode at the time, for often quite simple reasons. They were designed, with great skill and expense, to explode and kill. And that is what they can and sometimes will still do, if interfered with. Barely a year goes by without someone being killed by unexploded First or Second World War munitions. Leave their disposal to the French or Belgian authorities.

Beware. Even items such as deactivated shells etc. bought at militaria fairs can cause you problems with the authorities. Not all are properly deactivated. Relic rifles, for example, can be deemed under the strict British Firearm Acts as not legally deactivated. Many rusty and bent remnant guns,

Chapter 12

RESEARCH SOURCES AND TIPS

Preamble

The total male British population in July 1914 was estimated at 22,485,501 and by the Armistice well over 7 million had served their country in uniform. But not all served in a theatre of war. And not all were in the Army. The navy and air services too played a vital role. When adding overseas contingents and women that number rose to around 9 million. Statistics, even official ones, can be confusing and seemingly contradictory. Some men served in more than one theatre of war. Some were wounded more than once. A few important statistics are given in Chapter 10, but for enthusiasts, I recommend poring over the plethora of facts and figures crammed into the 880 large pages of the official statistics of the war (see Bibliography).

The introduction offers a few basic tips, amplified a little here. Whenever possible use primary sources of information, which can include family documents and medals. If anything is copied from the original, errors may appear. Sometimes, however, transcripts are all that remain available. Use all sources with caution for everybody makes mistakes.

What can be discovered from various service records? Unfortunately more is often available for those who died than survived. The best you can usually hope for are some basic facts and details of what the man's unit was doing at a particular time. There are of course exceptions to this, such as when an individual soldier is named in a book or official document, whilst playing a part in an action.

There are various excellent specialist books on researching military ancestors and I recommend consulting those shown in the Bibliography. This chapter can only be a summary. I have quoted various establishments, record series, etc. and then attached their popular abbreviated title for future use. As much information is continually being digitalized by official organizations and private companies, it is usually not practical to quote exact references for they often change. Instead, pointers to the type of information and most useful places to consult it are given. Exceptionally I have quoted the main class reference for major document holdings of The National Archives.

With the ever-expanding internet it is highly recommended you search it to see just what has been included. Most major relevant organizations, at home and overseas, have excellent sites that may help. Usually records that can be downloaded, either from commercial organizations or official sites such as The National Archives, have to be paid for. It is necessary to ascertain their current conditions and charges.

What do you Already Have?

The Army had forms for just about everything. Many families have some of these among their heirlooms and they can provide a lot of useful information to expand upon. The more you can initially ascertain, the more can be discovered. First World War medals are engraved with the surname, initials, rank, number and regiment of the recipient. And nearly all those who went to war were issued with them. Where are they now? Many silver war badges (see Chapter 2) were issued. Most can be traced back to the original recipient.

Were any souvenirs brought home and can they be identified? But beware of the badge collector. The badges may not have been officially issued to your relative. Don't jump to conclusions. It is worth questioning relatives and friends of veterans for he may have given them a souvenir, or told anecdotes you were not aware of, that can provide valuable clues to his service. Be sceptical, but nevertheless analyse everything you hear or see.

It was the deliberate policy not to bring home for burial the dead bodies of fallen servicemen. Very few indeed were repatriated. There were nevertheless special church services held in their honour by families and friends. It was common for 'In Memoriam' cards or books to be printed to remember the lost one's life. These cards are frequently found among family documents and can provide quite useful information.

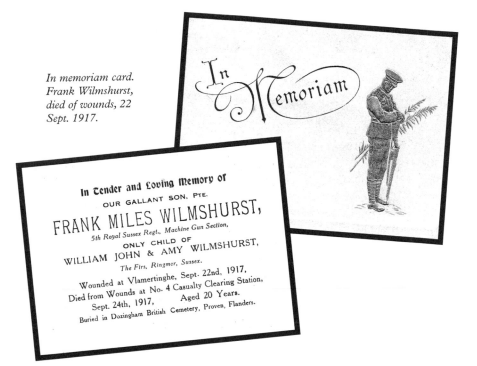

*In memoriam card.
Frank Wilmshurst,
died of wounds, 22
Sept. 1917.*

In Memoriam

In Tender and Loving Memory of
OUR GALLANT SON, PTE.
FRANK MILES WILMSHURST,
5th Royal Sussex Regt., Machine Gun Section,
ONLY CHILD OF
WILLIAM JOHN & AMY WILMSHURST,
The Firs, Ringmer, Sussex.
Wounded at Vlamertinghe, Sept. 22nd, 1917,
Died from Wounds at No. 4 Casualty Clearing Station,
Sept. 24th, 1917,   Aged 20 Years.
Buried in Dozingham British Cemetery, Proven, Flanders.

Well over 32,000 British soldiers died in the British Isles. A few were actually killed here in action fighting German warships bombarding our coastal towns. Many were brought home with a 'Blighty wound'. Some succumbed to their injuries. Other servicemen died as a result of accidents or disease. Bodies were washed ashore from ships and airmen crashed – often with fatal results. These and others were buried in Britain and many, but not all, have a Commonwealth War Graves Commission headstone. It is also not unusual to find an inscription on a family grave commemorating a member of the armed forces who died abroad. The body is not there but the soldier is nevertheless remembered. Sometimes the information, quite literally carved in stone, can be rather illuminating.

Photographs

It was common practice for soldiers to privately have their photograph taken in uniform as gifts to their family and friends. Many were

Many had their photographs taken privately before going to war. Sadly, this man, William Saunders, London Scottish, was killed on 1 July 1916.

photographed just before embarkation and usually indicate the soldier's regiment. Other soldiers had their pictures taken overseas during the war or when home on leave. Often the name and address of the photographer can be found, which may offer a clue to where the man was at the time. These photographs can tell us a lot if examined critically with a good magnifying glass and the insignia correctly identified from reference books. Badges etc. of rank, medals, skills, long service, wounds and regiment may be visible. The diagram shows where each should be located, but there are many anomalies and variations.

Very many photographs were taken during the war but relatively few are of use in researching family history. Most portray battle scenes, but many are in fact set in rear training areas and pretend to show action. To judge whether a photograph is genuine or staged consider the location of the photographer. If he was probably 'in harm's way' the picture was usually staged in some back area. If he was nicely shielded from enemy fire it may represent actual action. The official photographers used unwieldy and slow cameras, generally mounted on large tripods, and would have made a wonderful target. Portraits taken in rear areas can however be quite revealing as insignia on the uniform can tell us much about the soldier. Censorship was strict and in the fighting zones only approved photographers were allowed. However many unofficial snaps were taken on small (but prohibited) pocket cameras.

Colour photographs were very rare in the Great War but some do exist. They were mostly French and used the newly discovered Autochrome process for true colour. When analysing black and white photographs it is worth remembering that red appears darker than blue. To check this look at the roundels used on British and French aircraft. (The British had a red centre spot and blue outer ring – the French had the opposite arrangement.) It is useful to go to a museum and photograph as many exhibits as possible in both colour and black and white and judge for yourself how colours appear in shades of grey. (This is an easy adjustment with most digital cameras.)

Visible Insignia

If cap badges are clearly visible these can be identified to a regiment by reference to one of the many books available on the subject.

Rank

This is evident in the form of chevrons – often called 'stripes': they were worn, point down, on both upper arms. One stripe denoted a lance corporal, two a corporal and three a sergeant. There were naturally other ranks within the non-commissioned officer grouping, such as corporal of horse (equal to a sergeant), to confuse the unwary! Officers officially wore their rank insignia on both cuffs for much of the war

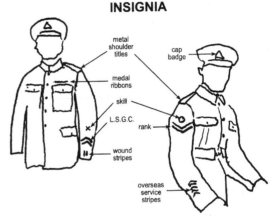

INSIGNIA

Sketch showing usual location of the various insignia.

before they appeared on the epaulettes. There were however many variations, partly depending upon the seniority and regiment of the officer. Most officers going into action wore standard Tommy's uniforms to disguise their status from enemy snipers.

Regiment

There were brass regimental titles, worn on both shoulder straps of the tunic and greatcoats, unless removed to hide the identity of the unit prior to a battle. Officers in field service dress did not usually wear them. Guards regiments had their regimental insignia embroidered into their uniforms.

Overseas Service Chevrons

These were introduced in January 1918 and a maximum of five were approved. They were worn inverted on the lower right sleeve of the tunic. The one for 1914, if appropriate, was coloured red and sewn nearest the wrist. All other years were represented by blue chevrons and sewn above it.

Long Service and Good Conduct (LSGC)
These inverted cloth chevrons were sewn on the left lower sleeve. One stripe equalling two years, two for six years, three for twelve years and four for eighteen years of, as many old soldiers used to say, 'undetected crime'.

Wound Bars
These were fixed vertically on the left lower arm below any long-service stripes. They were brass and fixed from behind the tunic material. Each wounding qualified for an additional bar and many men had several.

Skill Badges
These can appear on the top right or lower left arm depending upon their significance. Those for an instructor were on the right upper arm whereas skill at arms badges were worn on the lower left arm.

The National Archives (TNA)

Kew, Richmond TW9 4DU (www.nationalarchives.gov.uk/). Formerly called the Public Record Office (PRO), it is the main place to seek information regarding people who served in the Great War. A reader's ticket is required to consult original documents and their website gives full details. It also contains much useful information and I highly recommend that you consult it regularly for updated procedures on accessing records – some of which can be downloaded via the internet.

From time to time The National Archives enters into partnership with outside commercial organizations for the copying and resale of national records. This is an ongoing procedure and changes periodically. Check details of availability with the website.

Catalogue
The Catalogue (of their collection) can be accessed via the home page. An essential guide to TNA Great War records – what they are and how to use them – is *First World War Army Service Records* by their principal military adviser, William Spencer. There are also 'research guides', both at The

National Archives and available to see online, which give invaluable advice on many aspects of the collection.

Groups of records are commonly called classes. The National Archive classes begin with letters followed by numbers. After that a further number is allocated to each document or file within the collection. The main letter codes concerning us here are:

WO/War Office
ADM/Admiralty: (Royal Navy, Royal Naval Division and Royal Naval Air Service)
AIR/Air Force (Royal Flying Corps and Royal Air Force)
ZJ/1 *The London Gazette*: Announcements and citations for awards

Searching the 1901 Census will often provide useful information on names and family background. Wartime marriage certificates usually give the rank, number and unit of the groom. It is also possible to purchase a death certificate for anyone who died during the war but they rarely show much useful information. Commonly the cause of death is 'killed in action'. Civilian death certificates, issued in respect of men who had already been discharged from the forces, often contain greater information as to the clinical cause of death.

Medal Index Cards (MIC): WO372/

As detailed in Chapter 2, men and women serving in a recognized theatre of war were entitled to campaign medals. The entitlement is summarized on the MIC, which should be available for every qualifying officer and soldier. Each card gives a précis of the unit(s), rank(s), number(s) and regiment(s). On occasion extra notes, perhaps recording the death or entitlement to gallantry medals, were added. The card rarely shows unit details below the regimental or corps name. Sometimes this can be ascertained by examining the full medal rolls. Electronic copies of the MIC can be seen at The National Archives and may be downloaded from their website. Rather better, colour copies, showing both sides of the cards (many have extra information on the back – often showing where the medals were sent) can be downloaded from www.ancestry.co.uk. Usually the full name is given but not infrequently only initials appear. Beware; there may be more than one card for a soldier or officer. If the soldier was sent overseas before 31 December 1915 the card usually shows the first theatre of war he served in and the date he arrived there. Additional information is sometimes given for officers, including, on the rear, the *London Gazette*

There really was a Private Tommy Atkins. Typical medical index card.

references for successive promotions. If a soldier (or officer) did not serve in a theatre of war he was not entitled to campaign medals and there will be no MIC for him.

Campaign Medal Rolls: WO329/

The rolls are held by The National Archives and separate series cover the 1914 Star, 1914–15 Star, British War and Victory Medals, Territorial Force War Medal and Silver War Badge. These show the precise entitlement for each soldier and often contain additional information to that shown on the MIC.

Gallantry Medals

There are various lists but the usual place to begin is the *London Gazette* (ZJ/1). Consult the indexes for a reference to the actual gazette where the announcement appears. Detailed citations are given for major awards but it should be noted that there are none for the Military Medal. Sometimes other awards appear by name but no further information is published in the *London Gazette*. The study of medals is a specialist subject and there are many books available to help. Some of these, such as for the Distinguished Conduct Medal, include full citations and/or biographical information.

War Diaries

Each unit of battalion size or greater was obliged to keep a diary of events – from its perspective. Most but not all survive. Higher echelons such as brigades, divisions, corps and armies also kept diaries. Non-infantry units such as artillery brigades (but not usually batteries), engineer and service corps companies, casualty clearing stations etc. also kept diaries. There are literally thousands of them and most are housed at The National Archives under their reference WO95/. It is one of the most important collections concerning the Great War. Other ranks are rarely named in the diaries whereas officers regularly are. The smaller the unit, the more likely it is for a man to be named. Remember that any diary is only as good as the officer who wrote it. On a 'good day' it may be very descriptive. On a 'bad day' it may be very truncated indeed. It will nevertheless often give some idea what your relative etc. probably did on a day-to-day basis. Some diaries are being digitalized and made available through TNA website.

Service Records: Other Ranks

Most First World War army records were destroyed by fire during an air raid on the repository where they were kept in Arnside Street, London, on 8 September 1940. The majority that survived were damaged. They are in class WO/363 and referred to as 'burnt records'. It was vital that certain records, mainly for pensioners, were reconstructed from other government files. These are kept separately in class WO/364 'Unburnt records'. Both sets of records can be viewed on microfilm at The National Archives or via www.ancestry.co.uk. The information they show varies considerably but often includes attestation papers, conduct, military history and medical history sheets. The attestation documents usually contain much personal information, including a physical description of the soldier. An especially useful form is Army Form B103 (Casualty Form – Active Service). It summarizes basic details and records transfers, promotions, embarkations, leaves and injuries. The papers in 'unburnt records' often contain details of the injuries etc. resulting in the grant of a pension. Whilst the odds are not good, it is always worth searching the service records in the hope the ones you seek may have survived the fire.

Officers' Records

These were in three parts and typically only the correspondence section survives. Usually this consists of arguments over monies due the officer (or War Office). The records of service and confidential reports are mostly lost.

They are still interesting however and there are exceptions; so it is worth checking the files under classes WO/338 (index to WO/339) for Regular Commissions and WO/374 for Territorial Army officers. There are other classes covering small groups of officers. Consult The National Archives for details.

Other Records in The National Archives

It is also possible to obtain records of service of Royal Flying Corps, Royal Naval Air Service, Royal Air Force and Royal Navy personnel. Some of these can be downloaded from TNA website which give also full details of the various classes where the records are stored.

There are other records, too many and varied to cover in detail here, but unfortunately usually only samples remain; for example, pension records and medical records, the bulk having been destroyed over the years. Consult The National Archives for more information.

Soldiers with various visible insignia such as cap badge, medal ribbons, rank, unit, long-service and wound. The photographer's details are also visible.

Imperial War Museum

Lambeth Road, London SE1 6HZ (www.iwm.org.uk). There are other branches, including the former RAF airfield at Duxford where many aircraft and larger exhibits are housed. The website gives full details of branches and access to collections. This museum accommodates not only a vast amount of wartime artefacts but also a library of military books, maps, photographs, sound archives, films and other records, mainly concerning the two world wars. Their collections of documents, diaries and personal reminiscences, many deposited by or on behalf of veterans, are priceless.

Regimental Museums

These usually have extensive collections of medals and artefacts and tell the traditions of the regiment. Additionally they often have libraries which include copies of relevant war diaries, documents and correspondence with officers and men over the centuries. The files are rarely adequately indexed and it is worth contributing to regimental funds and befriending the curator – usually a fount of knowledge – to see just what can be found. The location of these museums can generally be found on the internet.

Army Lists

There are monthly and quarterly lists. The most useful are the monthly lists, which are indexed. It is possible to progress through them and follow an officer's career from commissioning, to any subsequent promotions, and also to see in which unit he served. It will not usually show temporary detachments to another unit. Copies are available in The National Archives, Imperial War Museum and National Army Museum.

Postmarks

The many postcards sent home during the war went through the British Army Postal Service. The postmarks are coded but can be translated to show from where the card was sent. See Bibliography for details.

Red Cross Lists of Missing

Each month the British Red Cross and Order of St John published an ongoing 'Enquiry List of [Officers and Soldiers Reported] Missing'. Those subsequently found or presumed dead were omitted from the next month's list but more were added as time went on. It is valuable, for unlike other sources, it usually shows not just the name, rank, number and battalion but also the man's company and platoon, together with the date he was posted missing. No complete run of these volumes exists but the Imperial War Museum probably houses the best surviving collection.

Voluntary Aid Detachments

VAD nurses came under the British Red Cross. Record cards of service during the Great War exist with the British Red Cross. Write to: Museum and Archives Department, British Red Cross, 44 Moorfields, London. EC2Y 9AL. Because of the time a search takes, please be prepared to donate at least £10.00 to the Red Cross.

County Record Offices

These sometimes house the records of the local regiment and also copies of the relevant war diaries. Using the constantly updated website 'Access to Archives' (A2A) hosted by The National Archives, it is possible to see what each record office holds.

Other useful documents include local newspapers, which are worth scouring for mention of actions involving your family, etc. Although there was strict censorship, that did not seem to prevent publication of often lurid accounts involving the deaths of the chums of the contributor. Families with several members serving commonly appear together with their stories and photographs. Also seen are lists of men enlisting from various schools and other establishments.

Trade and other directories may be helpful.

Voters' lists for 1918 are very useful. These will list as absent voters servicemen, aged 21 or more, serving in the armed forces at around October 1917 and, if it survives, an Absent Voters List itself will show the unit and regimental number of the man.

It is always worth checking local lists and card indexes to see if your man appears. Not everything will be catalogued on A2A.

Prisoners of War

A list is available (see Bibliography) of British officers taken prisoner which shows their name, unit, date missing, date repatriated and sometimes other information, such as where held or details of death. There is no complete list of other ranks captured and the records at The National Archives (WO/161) are incomplete, as are those few lists published over the years. It does seem however that over 195,000 British and Commonwealth officers and men were taken prisoner of war. A large proportion of these were captured during the March/April German Offensives of 1918. Although not so well publicized as for the Second World War, some prisoners nevertheless did escape and get home. The Red Cross in Geneva does have more information about prisoners of war. All applications must be in writing and include the full name, nationality and unit of the prisoner, plus any other details held. Because of other commitments, a long delay is to be expected and usually a substantial donation is expected. Write to: Archives Division and Research Service, International Committee of the Red Cross, 19 Avenue de la Paix, Geneva, CH-1202, Switzerland.

Soldiers (and Officers) Died in the Great War

This is the official casualty list for the British Army. It was originally published in 1921 in eighty-one volumes but has now been digitalized and can be examined in detail on CD-ROM. It is also available on the internet but can only be searched there by surname whereas the CD-ROM can be searched by any of its thirteen fields. These include, where the information is available, besides the name, regiment and battalion etc., the date of death, the places of birth, enlistment and residence, the rank and regimental number and often the man's previous service details. Using it one can extract precise details of who and how many were killed, when and in which theatre of war. The causes of death differentiate between killed in action, died of wounds and died. A few are more elaborate. The numbers and names of men from any particular town who died can easily be ascertained and there are many more features. It has huge potential for statistical research. The CD-ROM, *Soldiers Died in the Great War*, can be consulted at major reference libraries throughout the country or purchased from Naval & Military Press Ltd. It can also be viewed on their website www.military-genealogy.com or at www.findmypast.com.

Royal Naval Division

Extensive details relating to over 10,000 fatal casualties may be viewed online on at least two main family history websites. Use your search engine to obtain the current details.

Commonwealth War Graves Commission (CWGC)

2 Marlow Road, Maidenhead SL6 7DX (www.cwgc.org/). This most excellent organization is responsible for British and Commonwealth war graves and memorials of the two world wars and some other conflicts. They keep them to an extremely high standard. The most important purpose of their records is to provide information so that the next of kin may know the resting place or place of commemoration of their relatives. The CWGC records are therefore designed to identify the casualty and trace the cemetery or memorial. They give the location of the grave or memorial to aid a visit and thus provide a most valuable service.

The basic CWGC data consist of surname, initials, number, unit, date of death and burial or commemoration details. In 60 per cent of cases the next of kin supplied additional information, which can be most useful. The records can be consulted most easily on that organization's website. They also publish an excellent map showing the *Cemeteries and Memorials in Belgium and Northern France*.

Neither *Soldiers Died in the Great War* nor the records of the Commonwealth War Graves Commission stand alone. They complement each other with similar, but generally different, information other than the basic military identification details.

Published Sources

Both during and soon after the war many memorial books were published. Some contain thousands of entries. Initially some authors and organizations attempted to detail all the dead but soon gave up, as the task was just too big. In more recent times many books have been written, some containing extensive biographies and photographs, dedicated to 'local' men and women who made the ultimate sacrifice. Almost all are the result of extensive research and are truly labours of love. As some were published privately there is no comprehensive catalogue for them but generally enquiries, perhaps to the local Royal British Legion, should reveal where to find a copy.

Regimental histories and histories of various units of the army, navy and air services are another source of information and literally hundreds have been published. Many are long out of print but others are constantly being reprinted. Check your search engine to see just what is available.

War Memorials

These come in two main variations. Those on or near battlefields throughout the world commemorate the men who have no known grave. Memorials on shore to those lost at sea fill a similar role. Traditional war memorials at home (wherever that may be) honour local people who died in the war whether or not they have an identified grave.

Memorials on the battlefields to the missing are arranged in regimental order of preference, then by rank and then in alphabetical order. Local town or village memorials most often are in alphabetical order but other arrangements, such as date of death or rank order are not uncommon. Often there will be a companion memorial in a nearby church, village hall or library and it is worth checking for uniformity or extra information. *Arras memorial for flying services.* Don't forget stained-glass windows and separate plaques or memorials in or near churches. Cricket or football clubs, workplaces, etc., frequently contain more personal details and can be most informative.

The main naval memorials to their missing are at Chatham, Portsmouth and Plymouth. They are organized first in ship order, followed by rank then names. There are many other smaller memorials. The Merchant Navy is primarily honoured at Tower Hill, London – but again there are other memorials such as Hollybrook, Southampton. Missing airmen from the Great War are commemorated on the Flying Services Memorial at Arras, France.

The Commonwealth War Graves Commission can advise where any casualty is buried or commemorated on one of its memorials.

Records for who was included or excluded on local war memorials are uncommon as there was no national policy on this aspect of commemoration. It was left to local people to make these decisions, along with how to fund the memorial. Sometimes relatives of those who died did not want their fallen to be on the memorial and that wish was usually respected. Some men were not commemorated because their families had moved away. Surviving records of those named on the memorial can occasionally be located in the relevant county record office or local library but most seem to be missing. I suspect any still in existence are in the personal archives of the descendants of the then chairman of the war memorial committee. What are worth checking however are newspaper accounts of the unveiling of the local war memorial.

East Hoathly, Sussex. Typical of thousands of village war memorials.

At the ceremony it was the custom to place wreaths, along with a dedication card, to the family's fallen. After the ceremony the local newspaper reporter frequently copied down the details from those cards for publication in the next week's paper. Names in print sell newspapers! Find out when 'your' war memorial was unveiled and check the local papers.

There is a United Kingdom National Inventory of War Memorials being compiled under the umbrella of the Imperial War Museum. It is an ongoing project and more information, both on the memorials and those named on them, is constantly being added. The current web address is: http://www.ukniwm.org.uk/

One should not forget school, college, railway, post office, company or town hall records or memorials either. In short anywhere men were educated, worked, lived, worshipped or played may be a source of additional data.

Internet Family History Sites

It is well worth regularly checking exactly what the major family history sites have available. Three large ones, containing information especially useful to researching Great War dead are: www.ancestry.co.uk www.findmypast.com and www.military-genealogy.com Their collections increase all the time. Occasionally their name or web address may change, for the internet is a very fluid medium. It is however most unlikely that they will cease to trade. Any good search engine will find the latest location. From there see what is on offer and decide the type of subscription you wish to enter into. The major sites have sophisticated search facilities whereby you can enter brief identifying criteria and be taken to various sources of information within the entire collection.

Many local villages and parishes throughout the land have excellent websites covering local people, places and events. It is always worth trying to see what is currently available. I suggest initially entering on a search engine the parish where he or she was born, lived or died together with the name of the person you are researching.

Whatever digital sources you search I suggest there is one golden rule to adopt: 'less gives more'. I am also a great believer in the maxim of using a 'mark one eyeball and a modicum of commonsense'. If you search *Soldiers Died in the Great War*, for example, for my cousin 'Harold Bridger', who was killed in action on 18 November 1914, you will not find him. He served under the name of 'Harry Bridger'. If you had entered just his initial the record would have been displayed. Should your first search produce too many hits you can gradually eliminate those not required. If however the list does not include your relation then perhaps the assumption will be drawn that he is not there. That may not be true. It is worth using a little lateral thinking. For example at the time of the Great War the name 'Bert' was very popular. However, who was 'Bert'? He could have been Albert, Bertie, Bertram, Gilbert, Herbert, Hubert, Robert, Wilbert or even just Bert. There were over 65,000 men who perished during the War whose first names included 'Bert' in one shape or other. And was your William perhaps a Willie or a Bill? Much better to just enter a single initial to start with – assuming you are not looking for J Smith that is! Be careful with hyphenated names and also those containing an apostrophe. Mac can be awkward. It could be Mac or Mc and then there are variations on the capitalization of the next part of the name. Try each in turn for greater chances of getting a hit.

What's Left?

There are so many other minor sources of information that it is impossible to list them all here. Many archives in museums and universities hold material relating to the Great War. The books by Simon Fowler and Norman Holding referred to in the Bibliography detail many of them. Track down private collectors and enthusiasts near you with specialist knowledge. So many people are interested in the Great War that collectively, their knowledge base is truly awesome. There are also several forums, some hosted by the Western Front Association, that you could join and ask your question.

Postscript

Don't reinvent the wheel but remember there is no such thing as perfect research and the ultimate answer. More records become available as time goes on, although some are occasionally still being destroyed. There is usually more to be discovered – keep researching and good luck.

BIBLIOGRAPHY

General Books on the Great War

Abbott, P E and Tamplin, J M A. *British Gallantry Awards* (London: Nimrod, Dix & Co., 1981).

Banks, Arthur. *Military Atlas of the First World War* (London: Heinemann Educational Books Ltd, 1975).

Baynes, John. *Morale: A Story of Men and Courage* (London: Cassell & Co. Ltd, 1967).

Bridger, Geoff. *The Battle of Neuve Chapelle* (Barnsley: Leo Cooper, Barnsley, 2000).

Bull, G V and Murphy, C H. *The Paris Guns and Project Harp* (Herford and Bonn: Verlag E S Mittler & Sohn, 1988).

Chasseaud, Peter. *Artillery's Astrologer: A History of British Survey and Mapping on the Western Front 1914–1918* (Lewes: Mapbooks, 1999).

Fraser, Edward and Gibbons, John. *Soldiers and Sailors Words and Phrases* (London, 1925).

Hogg, Ian and Thurston, L F. *British Artillery Weapons and Ammunition 1914–1918* (London: Ian Allen, 1972).

Jäger, Herbert. *German Artillery of World War One* (Marlborough: Crowood Press, 2001).

James, Edward A. *A Record of the Battles and Engagements of the British Armies in France and Flanders 1914–1918* (Aldershot, 1924); *British Regiments 1914–1918* (London: Samson Books Ltd, 1978; combined edition).

Lewis, Captain Cecil. *Sagittarius Rising* (London: Peter Davies Ltd, 1936).

Oram, Gerald. *Death Sentences Passed by Military Courts of the British Army 1914–1918* (London: Boutle Publishers, 1998).

Petre, F, Ewart, W and Lowther, C. *The Scots Guards in the Great War 1914–1918* (London: John Murray, 1925).

Proud, E B. *History of British Army Postal Service*, vol 2. *1903–1927* (Dereham: Proud-Bailey Co. Ltd, 1983).

Rawling, Bill. *Surviving Trench Warfare* (Toronto: University of Toronto Press, 1992).

Simpkins, Peter. *Kitchener's Army* (Manchester: Manchester University Press, 1988).

Strachan, Hew. *The First World War* (London: Simon & Schuster, 2003)

Williamson, Howard. *Collector and Researchers Guide to the Great War*: pt 1. *Medals*; pt 2. *Small Arms, Munitions, and Militaria* (Harwich: Anne Williamson, 2003).

Young, Michael. *Army Service Corps* (Barnsley: Pen & Sword, 2000).

Books Useful for Researching Military Genealogy

Fowler, Simon. *Tracing your Army Ancestors* (Barnsley: Pen & Sword, 2006).

Fowler, Simon. *Tracing your First World War Ancestors* (Newbury: Countryside Books, 2003).

Hobson, Chris. *Airmen Died in the Great War 1914–1918* (Suffolk: J B Hayward & Son, 1995).

Holding, Norman. *World War 1 Army Ancestry* (Bury: Federation of Family History Societies, 2003).

Holding, Norman. *Location of British Army Records 1914–1918* (Bury: Federation of Family History Societies, 1999).

Holding, Norman. *More Sources of World War 1 Army Ancestry* (Bury: Federation of Family History Societies, 1998).
List of British Officers taken prisoner in the various Theatres of War between August, 1914 and November 1918 (London: Cox & Co., 1919).
Spencer, William. *First World War Army Service Records* (London: The National Archives, 2008).

Official Publications
Field Artillery Training 1914 (London: War Office, 1914).
Field Service Pocket Book 1914 (London: War Office, 1914).
Infantry Training 1914 (London: War Office, 1914).
King's Regulations and Orders for the Army 1912 (London: HMSO, 1912 and amendments).
Location of Hospitals and Casualty Clearing Stations, British Expeditionary Force 1914–1919 (London: Ministry of Pensions, c.1923).
Manual of Military Law (London: War Office, 1914).
Official History of the War: Military Operations: France and Belgium (14 vols plus appendices and map vols; London: various authors on behalf of Committee of Imperial Defence, various dates). (Similar Official Histories exist for other theatres of war and other arms of service.)
Order of Battle of Divisions, compiled by Major A F Becke (5 vols; London: HMSO, 1935–45).
Order of Battle of Divisions [Dominions, etc.], compiled by F Perry (2 vols; Malpas, Gwent: Ray Westlake – Military Books, 1992).
Order of Battle of the British Armies in France [at] November 11th 1918 (London: GHQ, 1918).
Statistics of the Military Effort of the British Empire during the Great War 1914–1920 (London: War Office, 1922).
Textbook of Small Arms 1929 (London: HMSO, 1929).
The Army List (London: War Office, monthly throughout the war).
The London Gazette (also *Edinburgh* and *Belfast Gazettes*) (London: HM Government, regularly throughout the war).
Vocabulary of German Military Terms and Abbreviations (London: War Office, 1918).

Organizations
Web addresses current at date of publication:
    Western Front Association: *http: //www.westernfrontassociation.com/*
    Gallipoli Association: *http://www.gallipoli-association.org/*
    Orders and Medals Research Society: *http://www.omrs.org.uk/*
    Cross and Cockade International: *http://www.crossandcockade.com/*

Digital Sources
British Trench Map Atlas (Uckfield: Naval & Military Press, 2008).
LinesMan [Trench maps] (Orpington: Great War Digital Ltd (Memory Map), 2007).
Soldiers Died in the Great War (Uckfield: Naval & Military Press, 1998).

Websites
Because of the ever-changing nature of the internet I am reluctant to recommend many unofficial websites. Some are excellent and improve over the years. Others fade away. Others change their name and consequently amend their web address. In addition organizations often amend their mailing address when secretaries etc. change. The better sites remaining current will usually appear on the first few pages of a good search engine and common sense should tell you the quality of the site you are viewing. Generally the more bibliographical references and fewest advertisements for unrelated material the better the site will be.

INDEX

Bold type is used for the main discussion of a topic and *italic* for illustrations.